OOGLEMAN

The Superhero Dragon

By Kendra Kessel

Illustrated by Vic Guiza

OOGLEMAN: The Superhero Dragon
Copyright © 2023 Kendra Kessel

First Edition

Written by: Kendra Kessel
Illustrated by Vic Guiza

www.FitHeroes.com
www.KendraKessel.com (Author's Website)

Published by:
Fit Heroes LLC
46 Peninsula Center Ste E. #505
Rolling Hills Estates, CA 90274

Library of Congress Control Number: 2023908730

Print ISBN: 978-0-9969373-3-7
eBook ISBN: 978-0-9969373-4-4
Print and creative services provided by www.vicguizaart.com

This book is dedicated to
Zander and Aria.
I love you so much and am so proud
to be your mom.

This book is also dedicated to you,
the reader. Your kindness, unique
personality, and special talents
make you a true superhero!

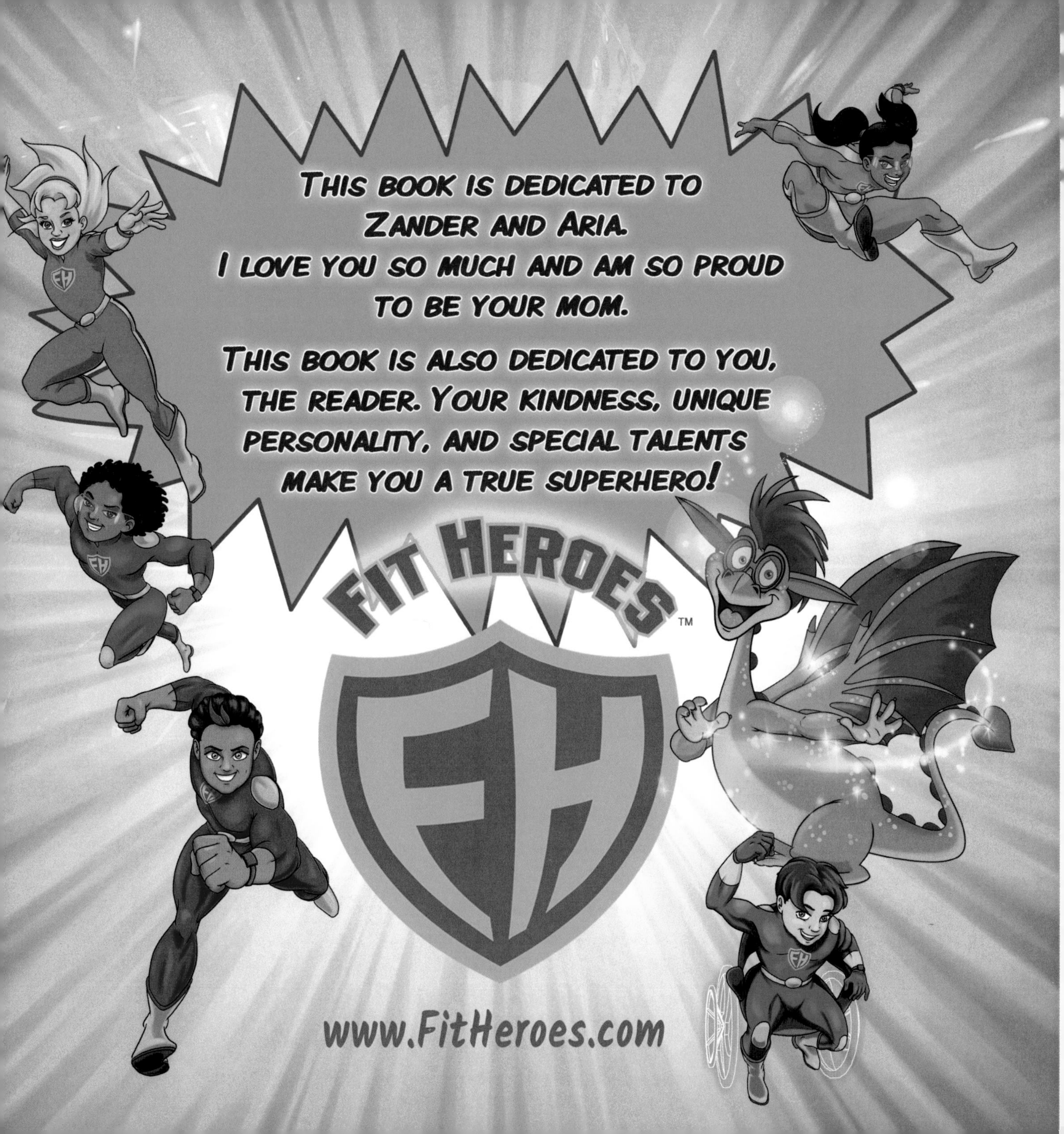

www.FitHeroes.com

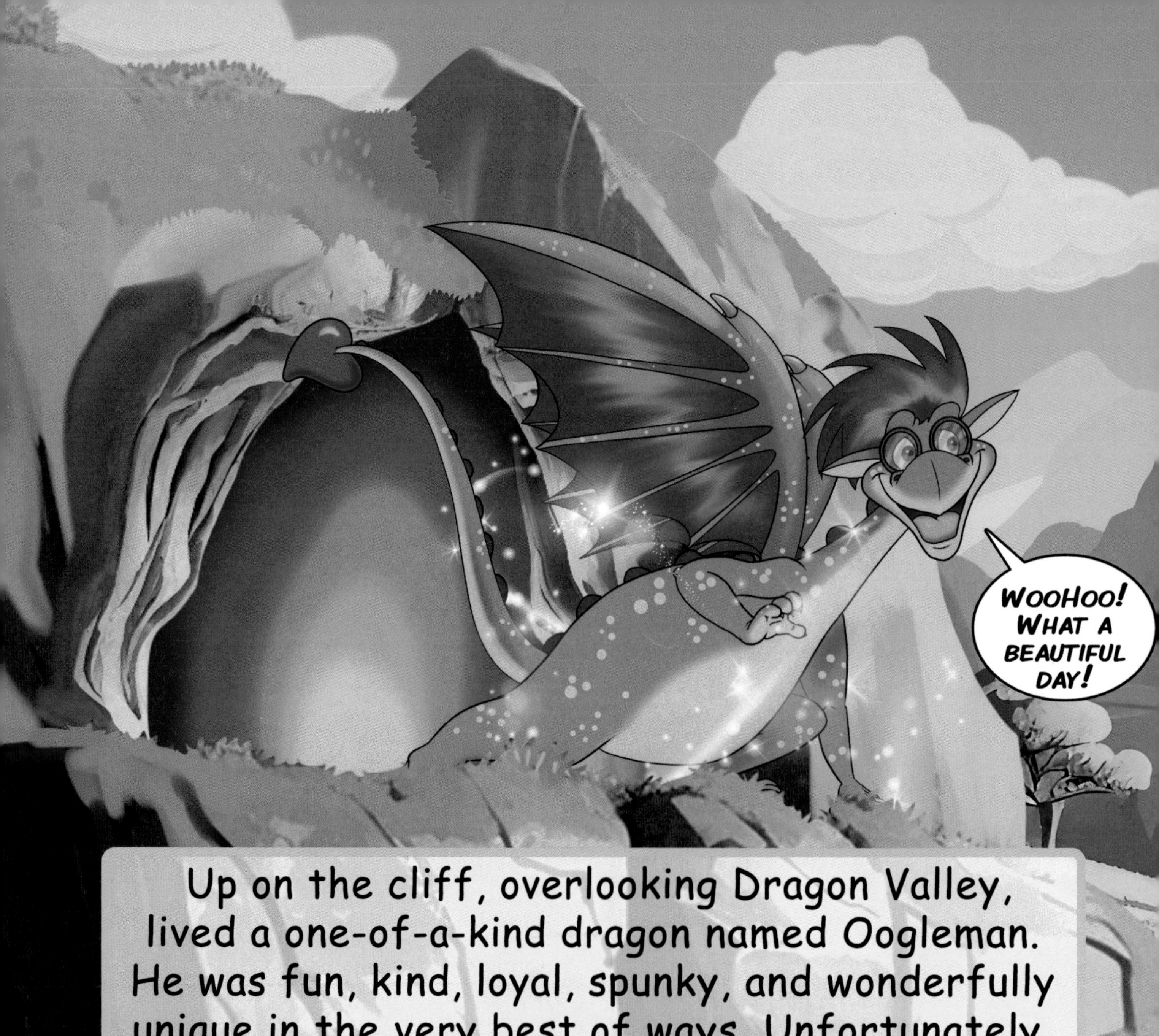
WOOHOO! WHAT A BEAUTIFUL DAY!

Up on the cliff, overlooking Dragon Valley, lived a one-of-a-kind dragon named Oogleman. He was fun, kind, loyal, spunky, and wonderfully unique in the very best of ways. Unfortunately, Oogleman couldn't seem to make friends or fit in anywhere, and he felt lonely.

People were scared of him, and dragons didn't want to be friends with him because he didn't look or act like them.
However, Oogleman knew that if he stayed true to himself, he would one day make friends with others who would accept him for who he was.

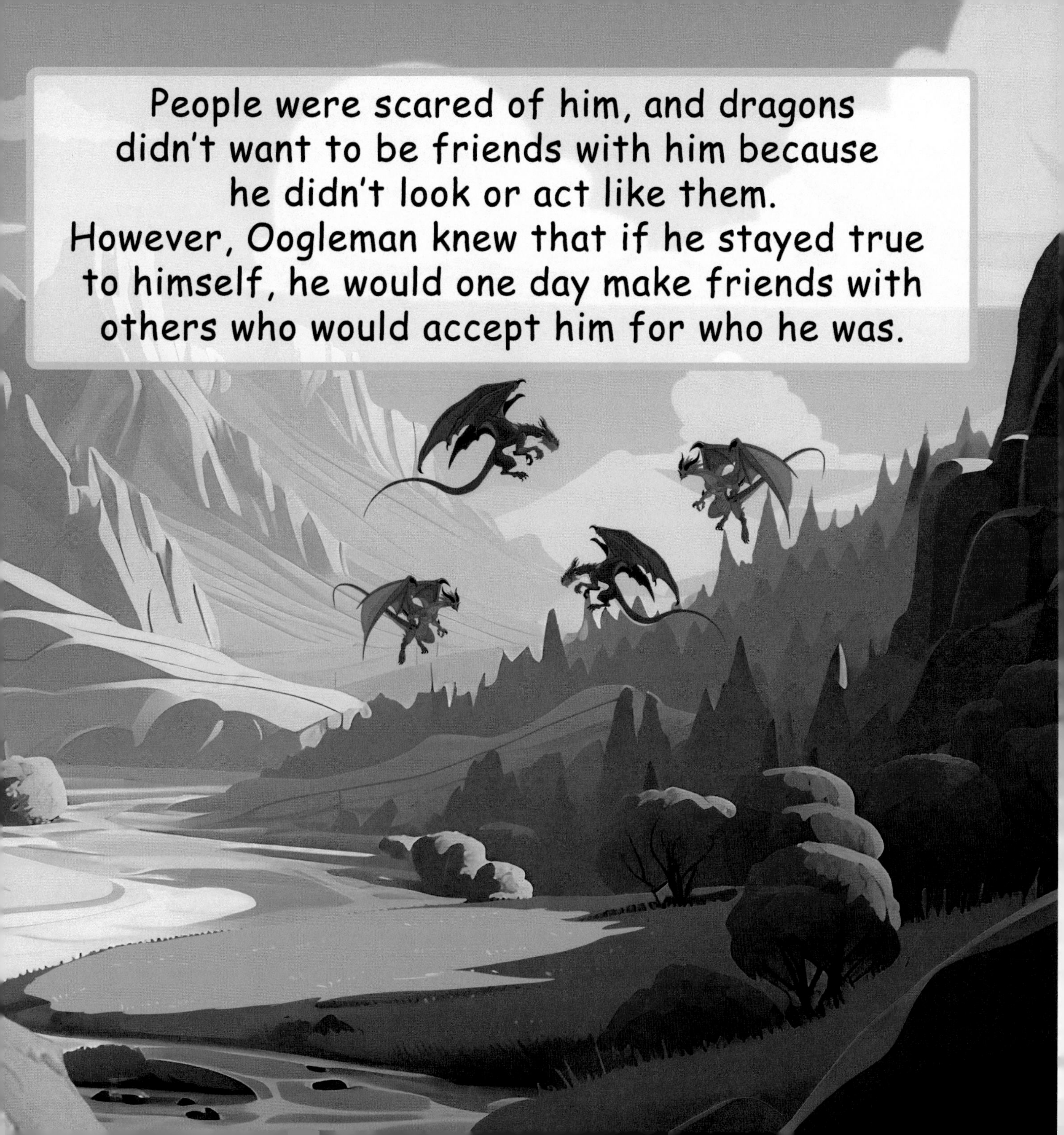

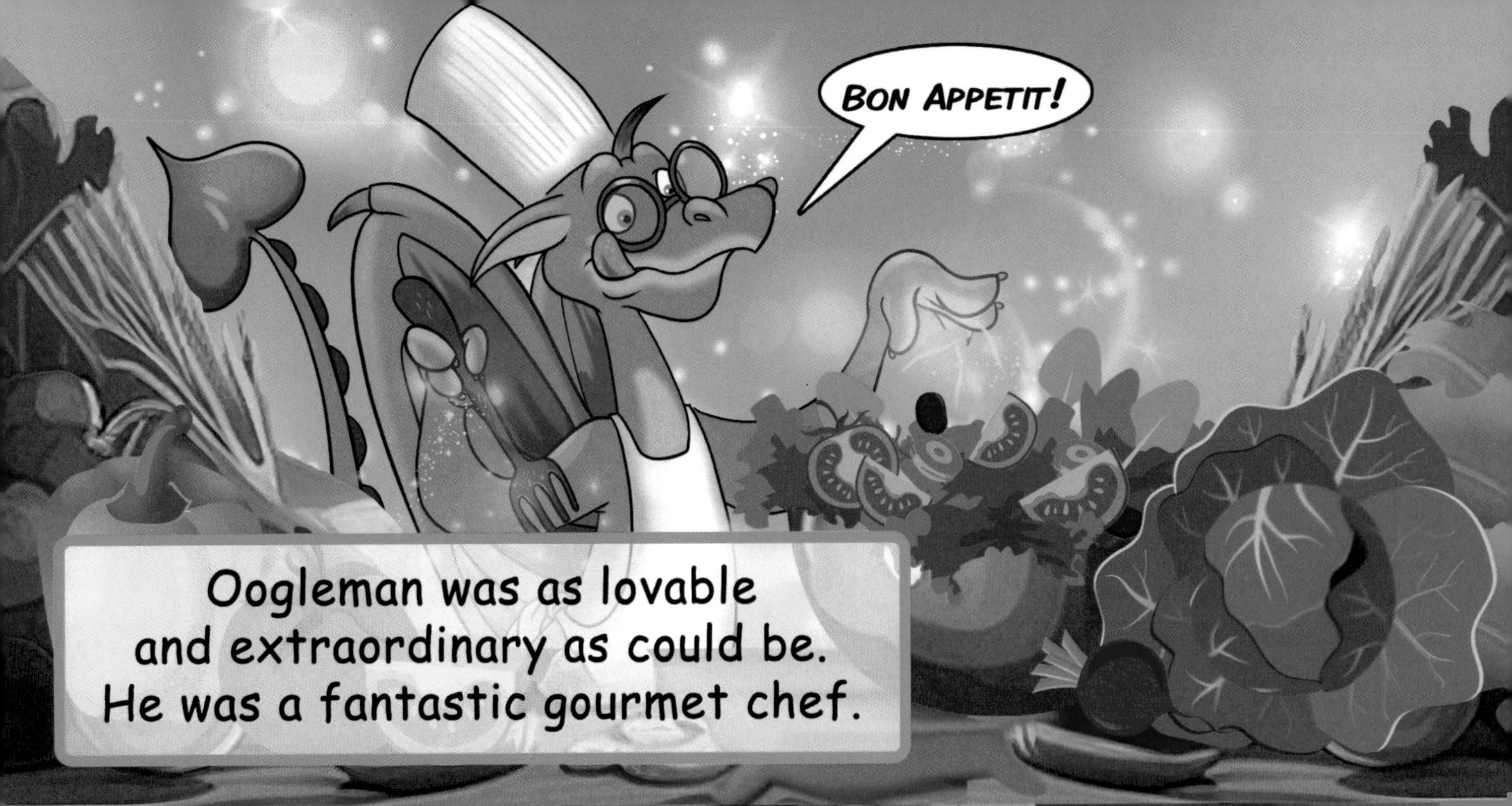
BON APPETIT!
Oogleman was as lovable and extraordinary as could be. He was a fantastic gourmet chef.

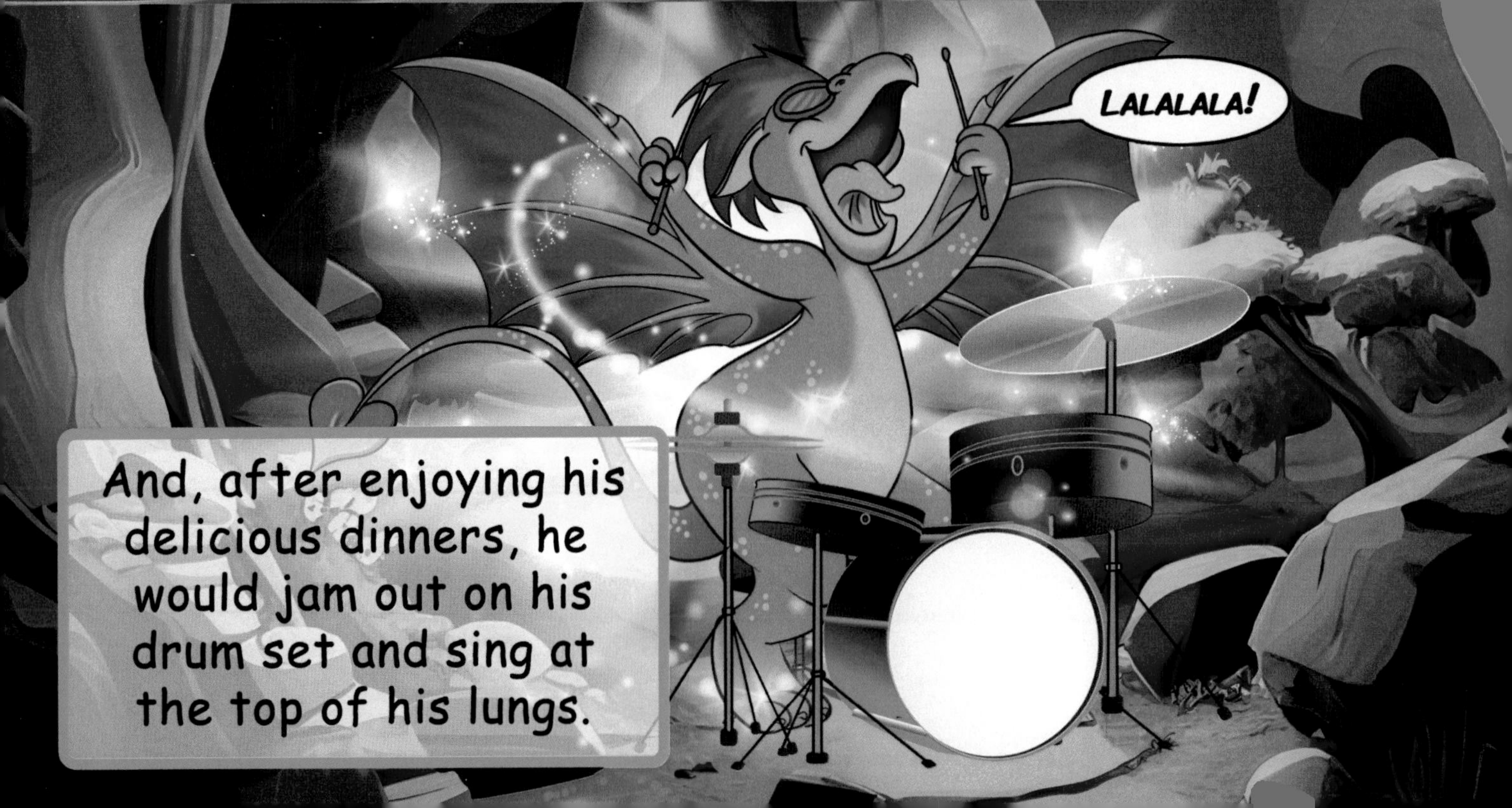
LALALALA!
And, after enjoying his delicious dinners, he would jam out on his drum set and sing at the top of his lungs.

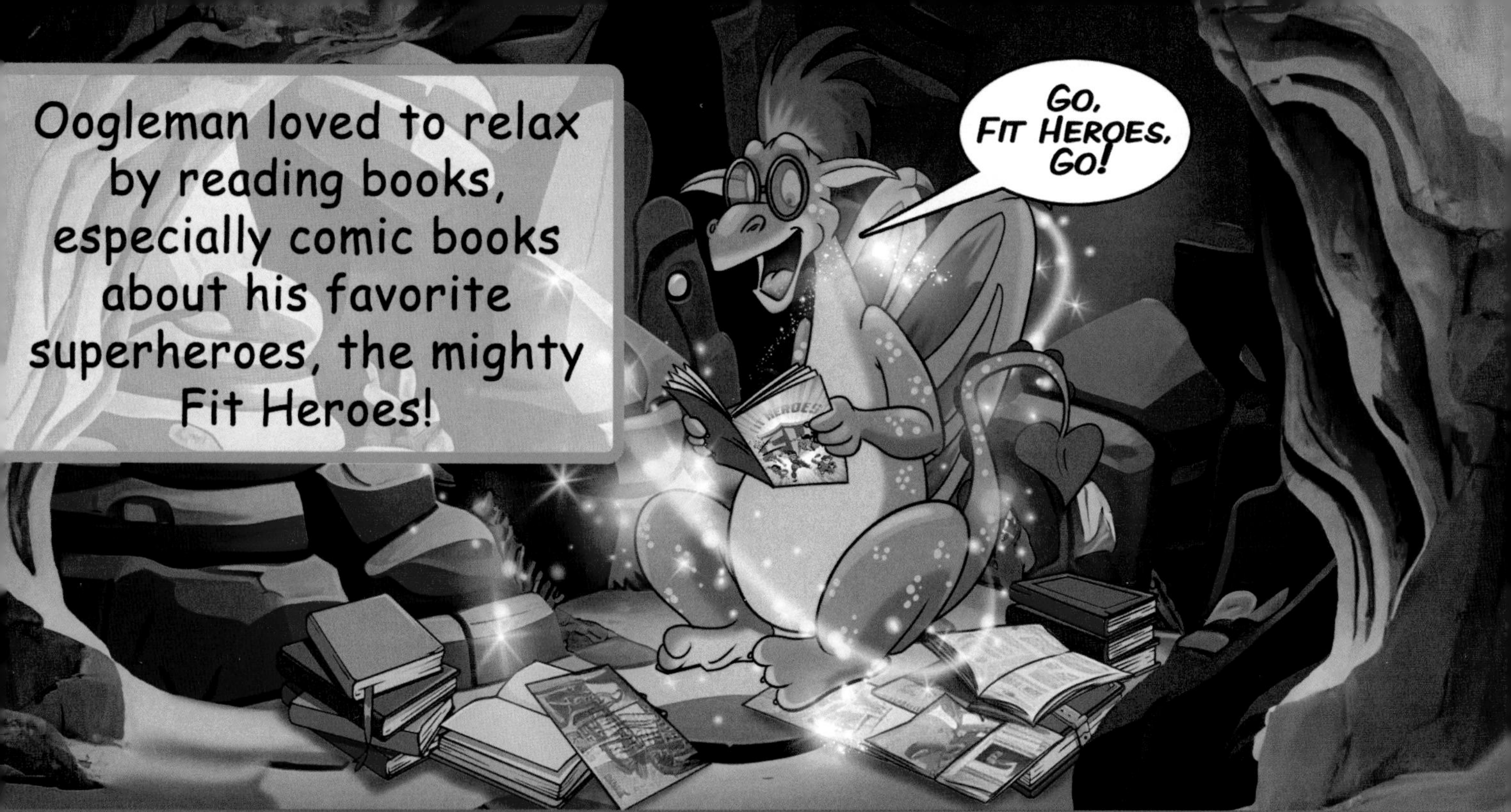
Oogleman loved to relax by reading books, especially comic books about his favorite superheroes, the mighty Fit Heroes!
GO, FIT HEROES, GO!

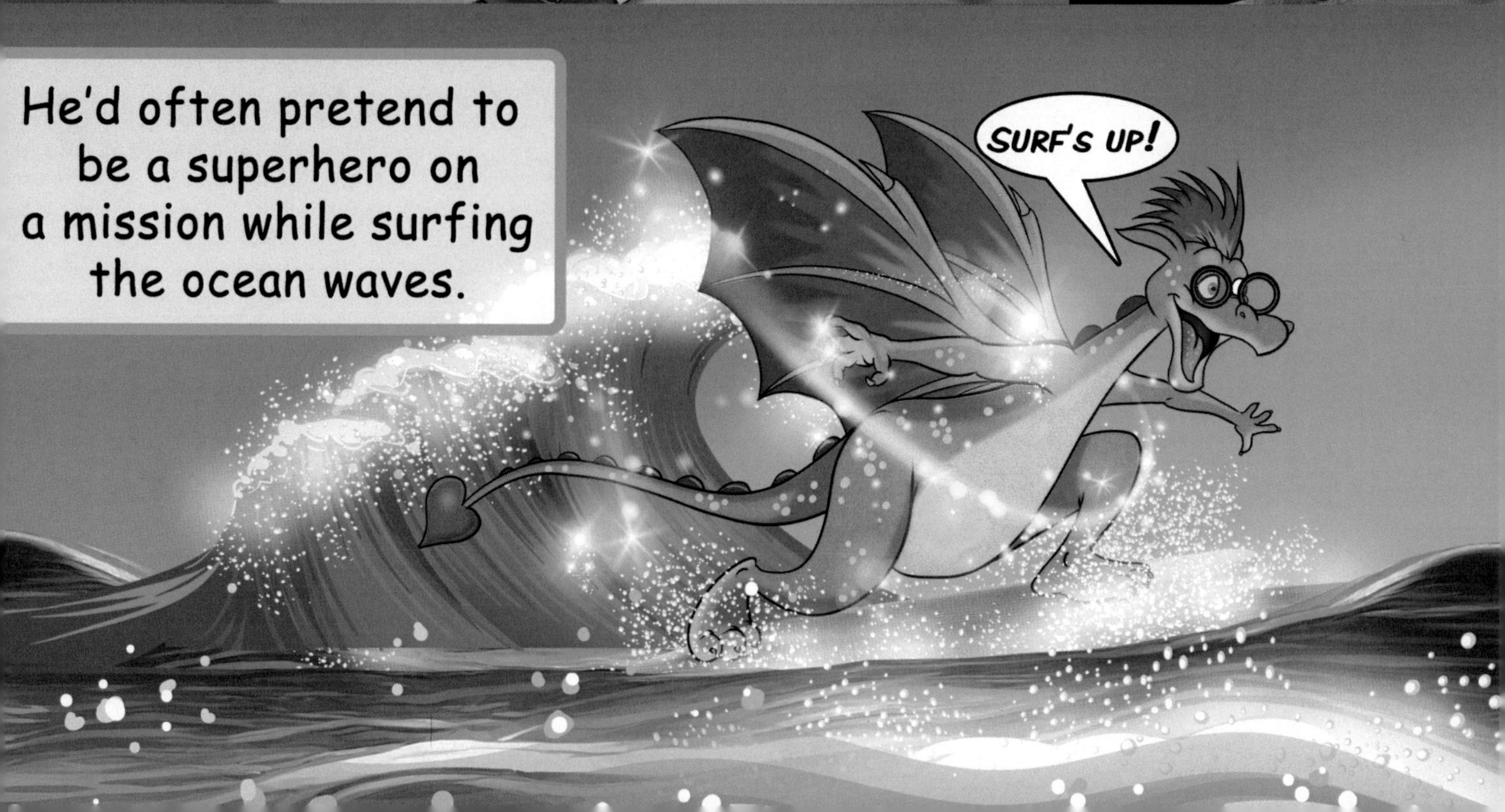
He'd often pretend to be a superhero on a mission while surfing the ocean waves.
SURF'S UP!

One evening, Oogleman was sleeping in his dragon's lair when he smelled something delicious in the air. He poked his head out and saw five kids roasting marshmallows by the campfire.

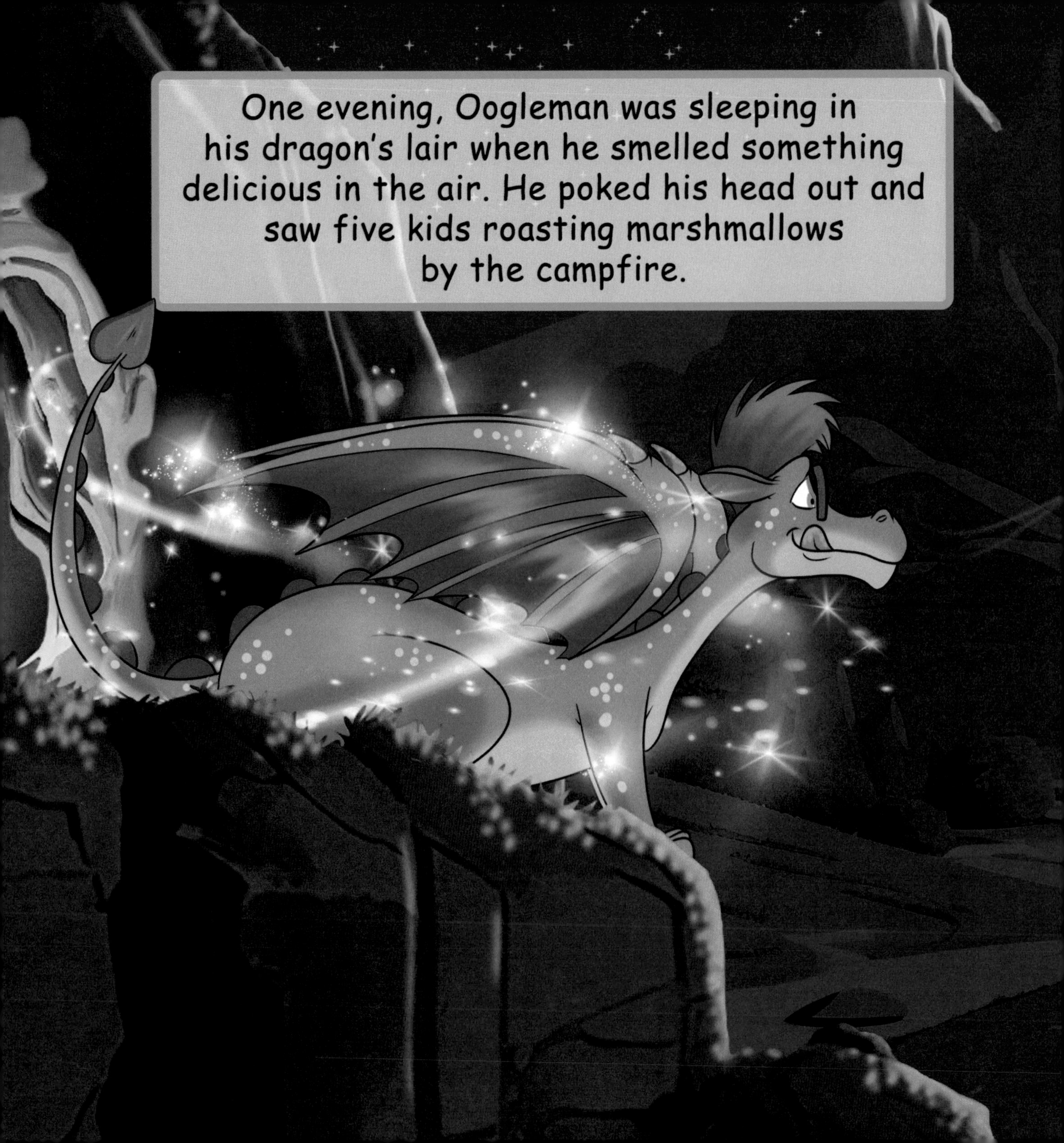

As he inched closer, Oogleman realized that they looked familiar. Wow! They were the mighty Fit Heroes – the coolest kid superheroes on the planet! He just had to meet them, but would they be scared of him like the other people were?
There was only one way to find out.

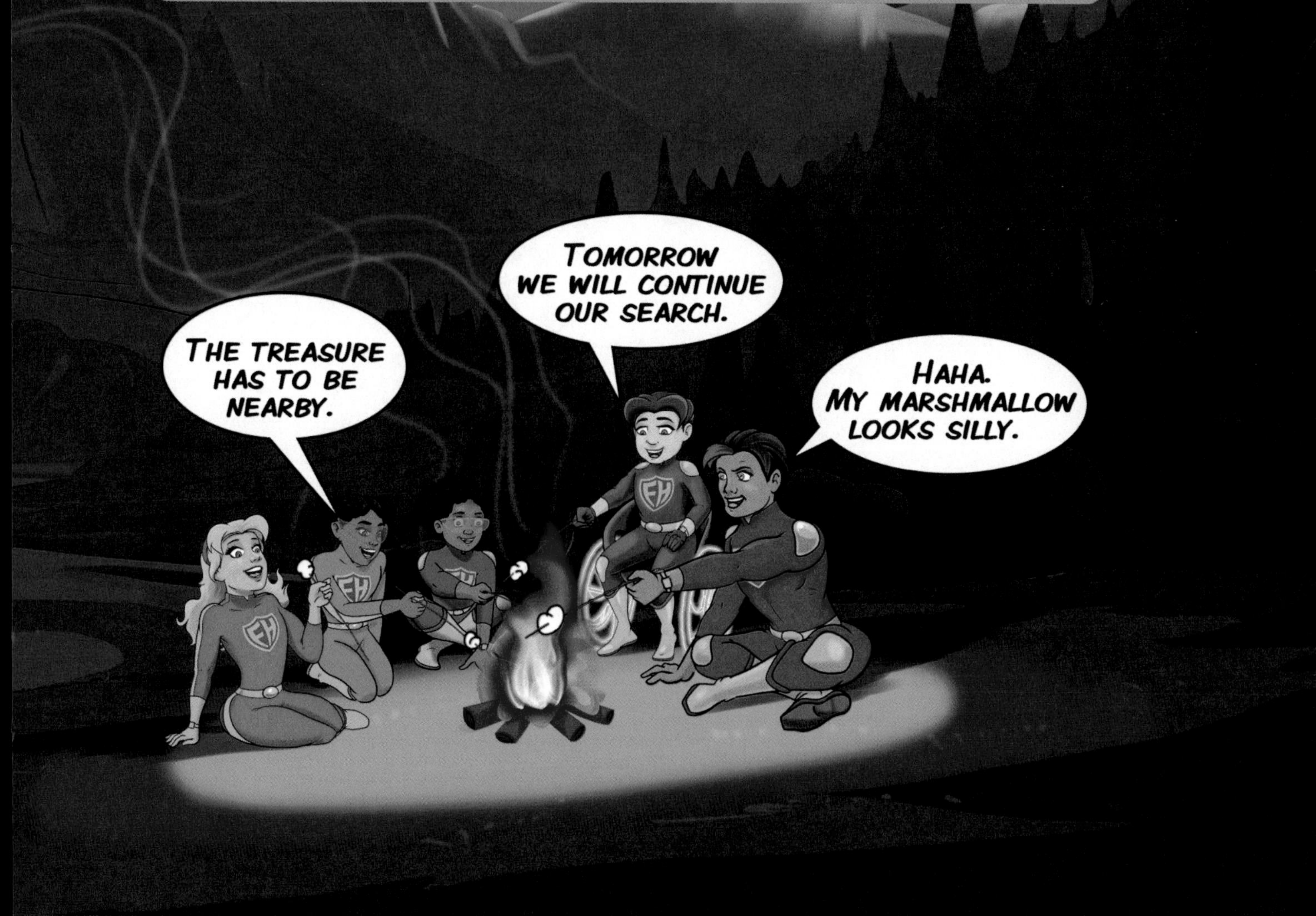
THE TREASURE HAS TO BE NEARBY.
TOMORROW WE WILL CONTINUE OUR SEARCH.
HAHA. MY MARSHMALLOW LOOKS SILLY.

Oogleman quickly gathered a basketful of fruits and vegetables and made his way towards the Fit Heroes to give them this friendly gift. He nervously approached them, unsure of how they would react to him. After all, he was a fire-breathing dragon.

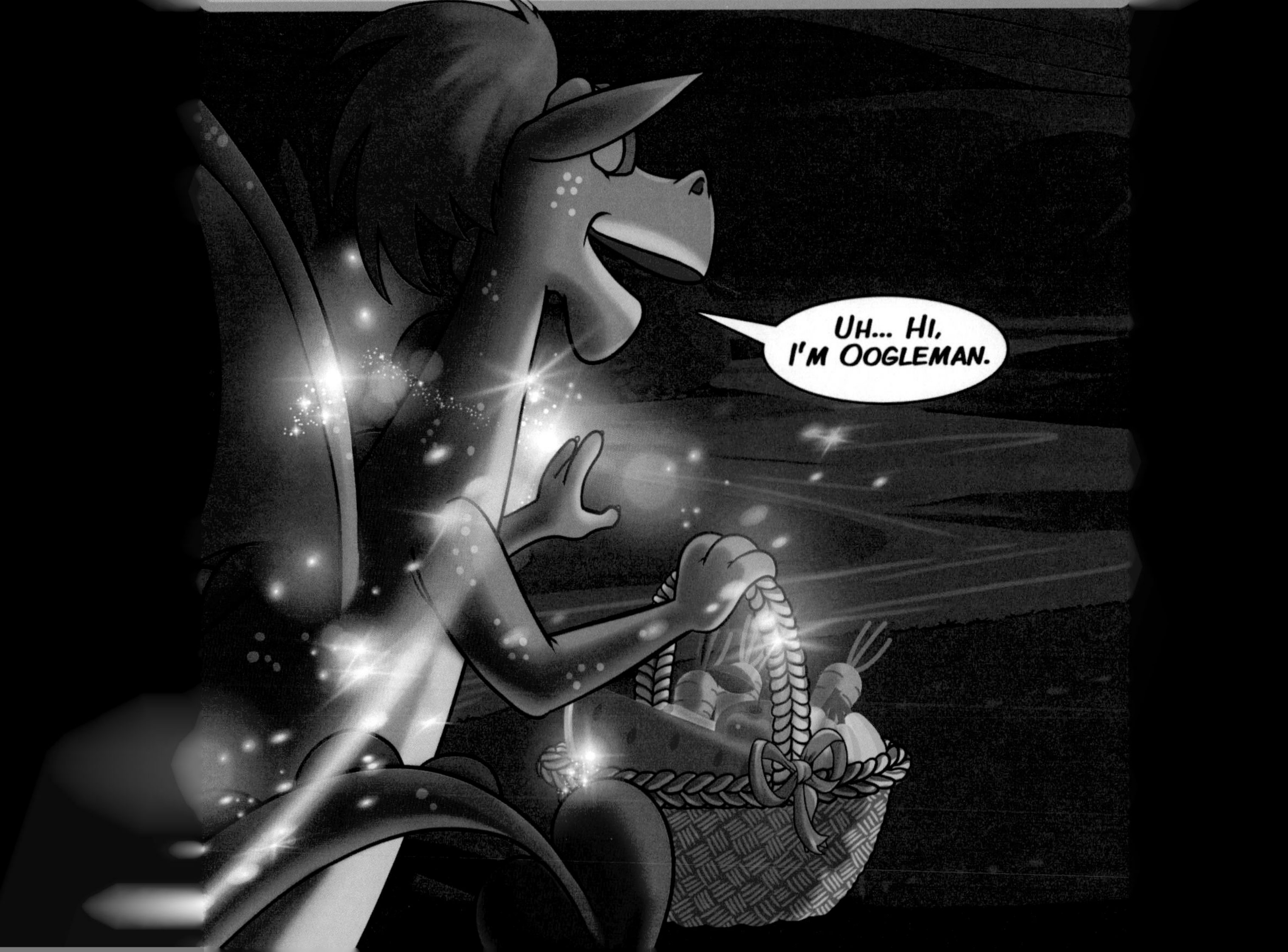
UH... HI, I'M OOGLEMAN.

The Fit Heroes heard a noise by the riverbank, and much to their surprise saw a big dragon walking towards them. However, they weren't scared at all. They could sense that he was kind and gentle.

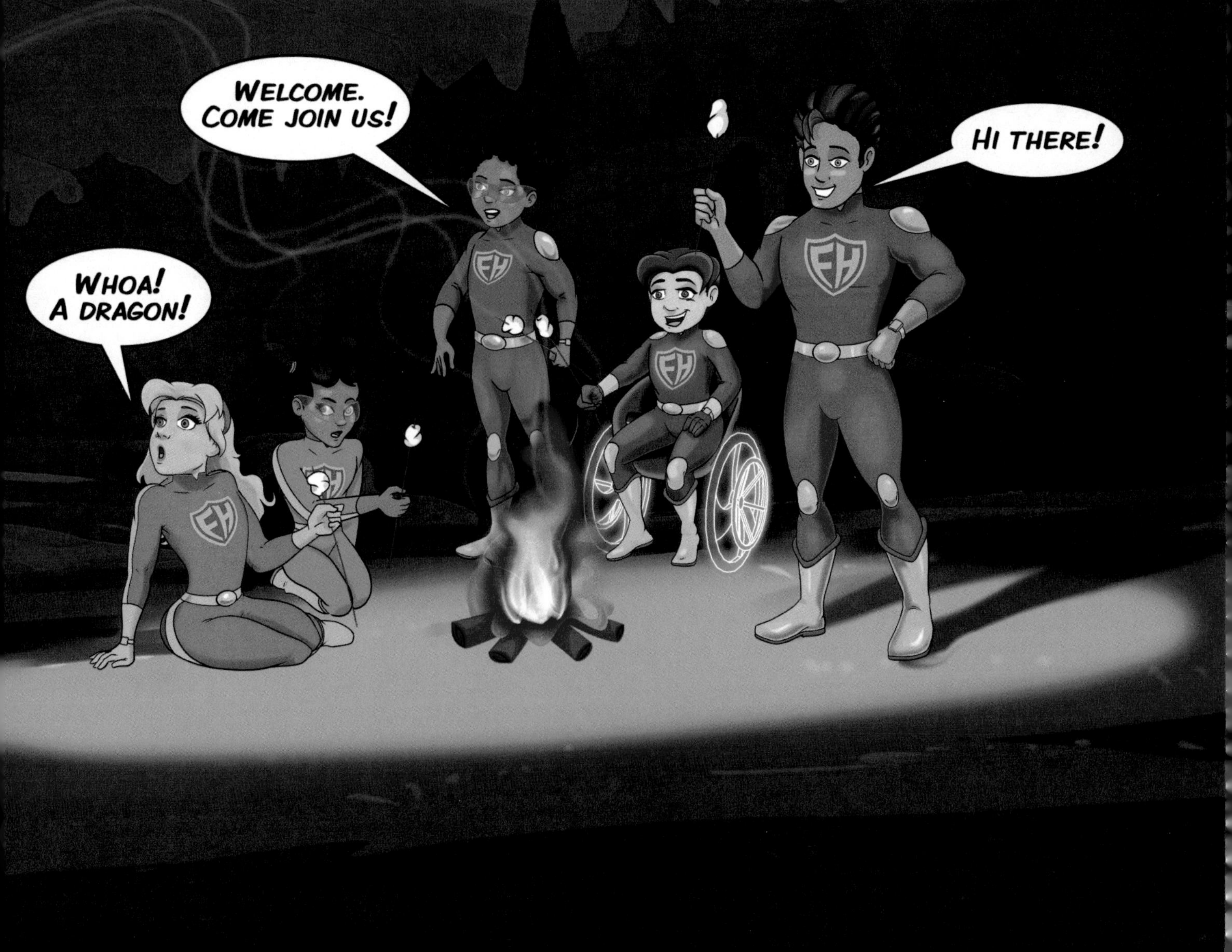
WHOA! A DRAGON!
WELCOME. COME JOIN US!
HI THERE!

That evening was the most fun Oogleman had ever had in his entire dragon life! They all enjoyed roasting marshmallows, telling stories, singing songs, and playing fun games. The Fit Heroes told him all about their mission.

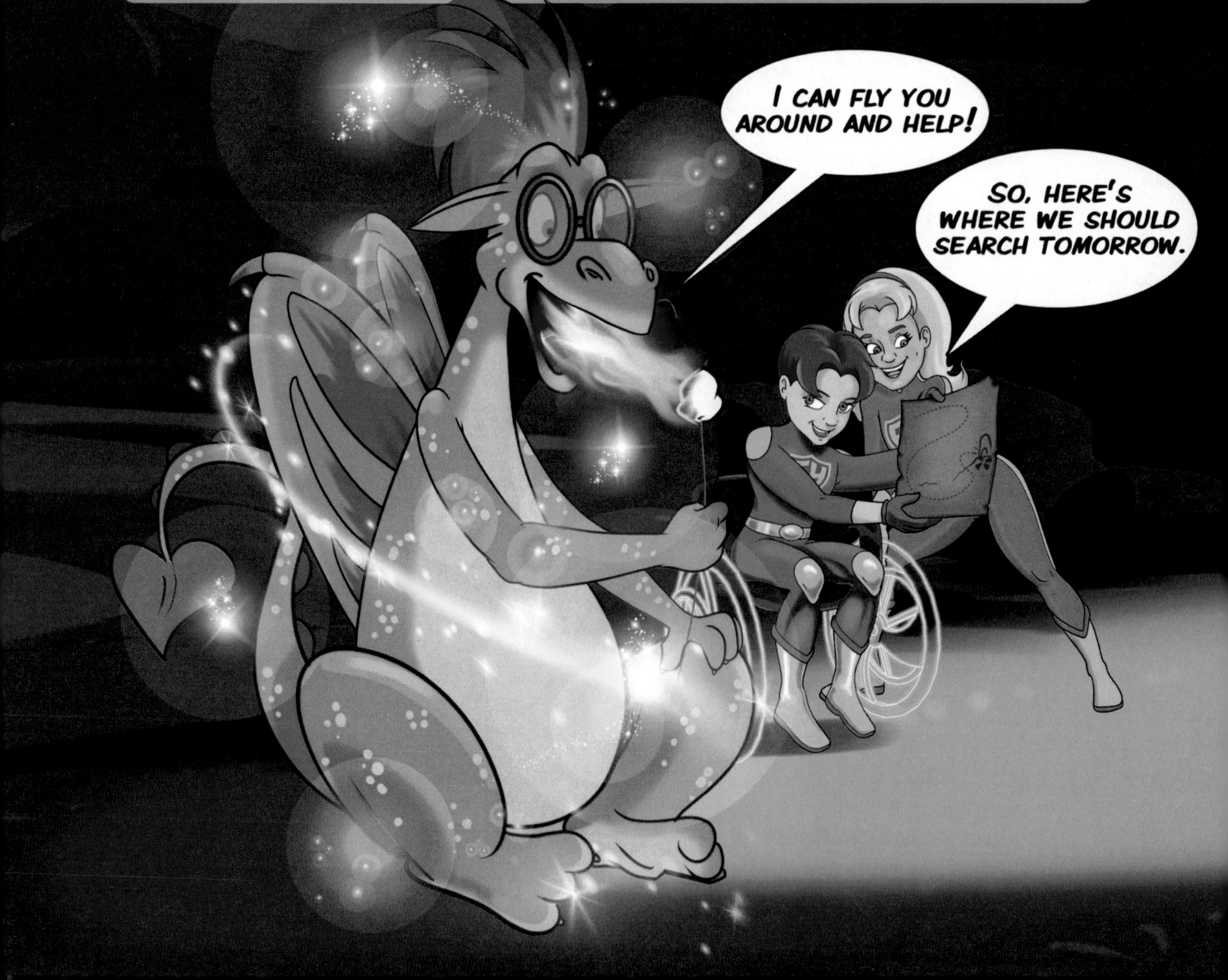

I CAN FLY YOU AROUND AND HELP!
SO, HERE'S WHERE WE SHOULD SEARCH TOMORROW.

They had found a secret treasure map that had led them to Dragon Valley. Now, they were trying to find the Hidden Gems Cave, supposedly filled with magnificent treasures. Oogleman beamed with excitement and proudly offered to help them find the treasures in any way he could.

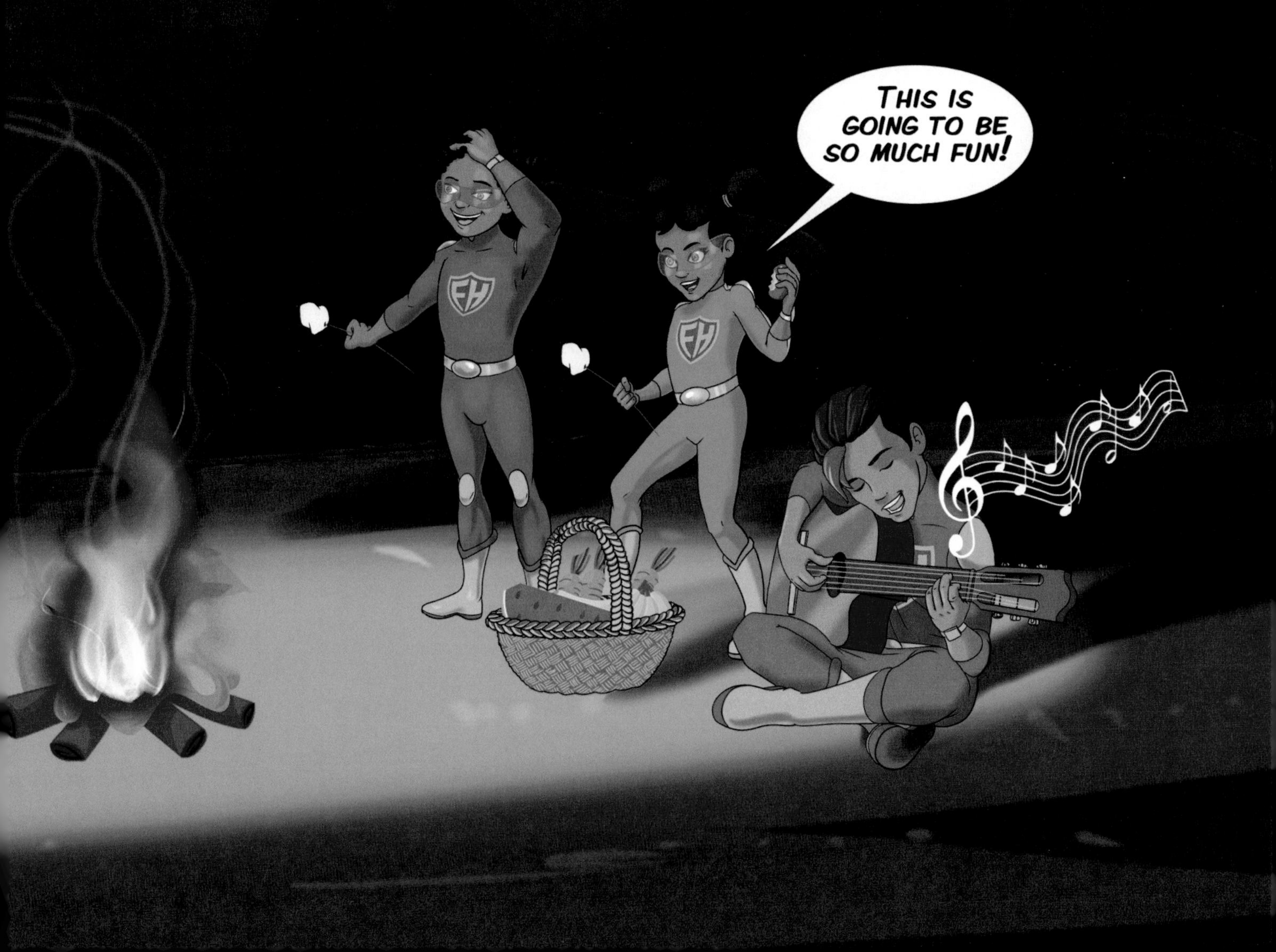
THIS IS GOING TO BE SO MUCH FUN!

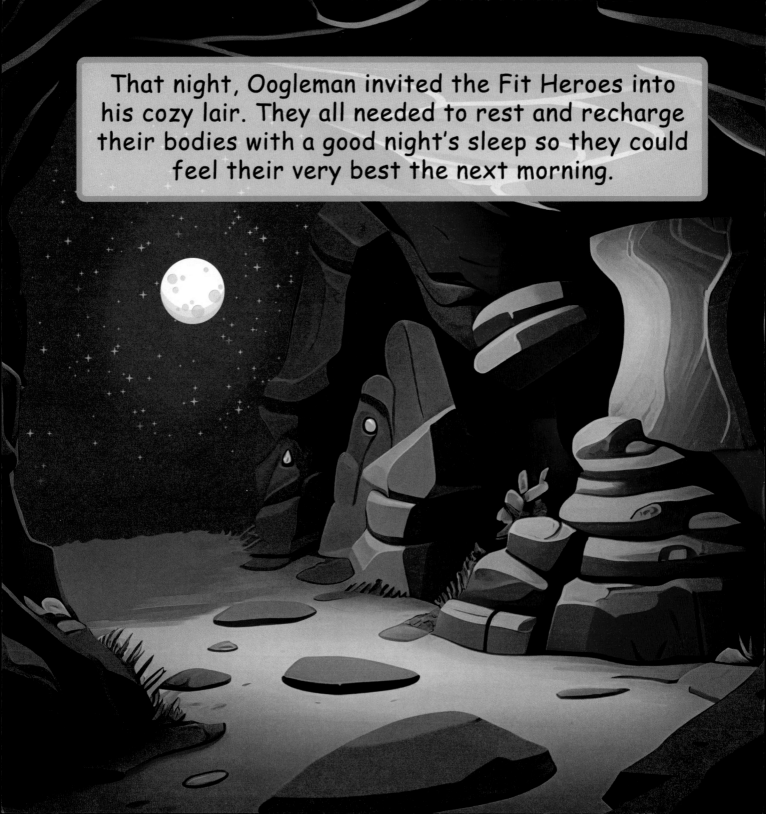

That night, Oogleman invited the Fit Heroes into his cozy lair. They all needed to rest and recharge their bodies with a good night's sleep so they could feel their very best the next morning.

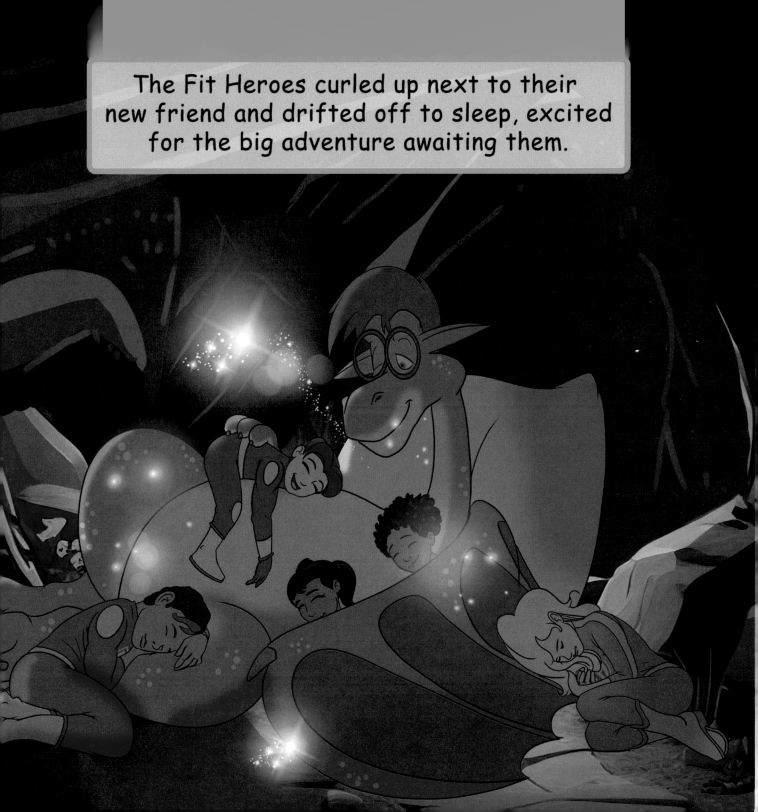

The Fit Heroes curled up next to their new friend and drifted off to sleep, excited for the big adventure awaiting them.

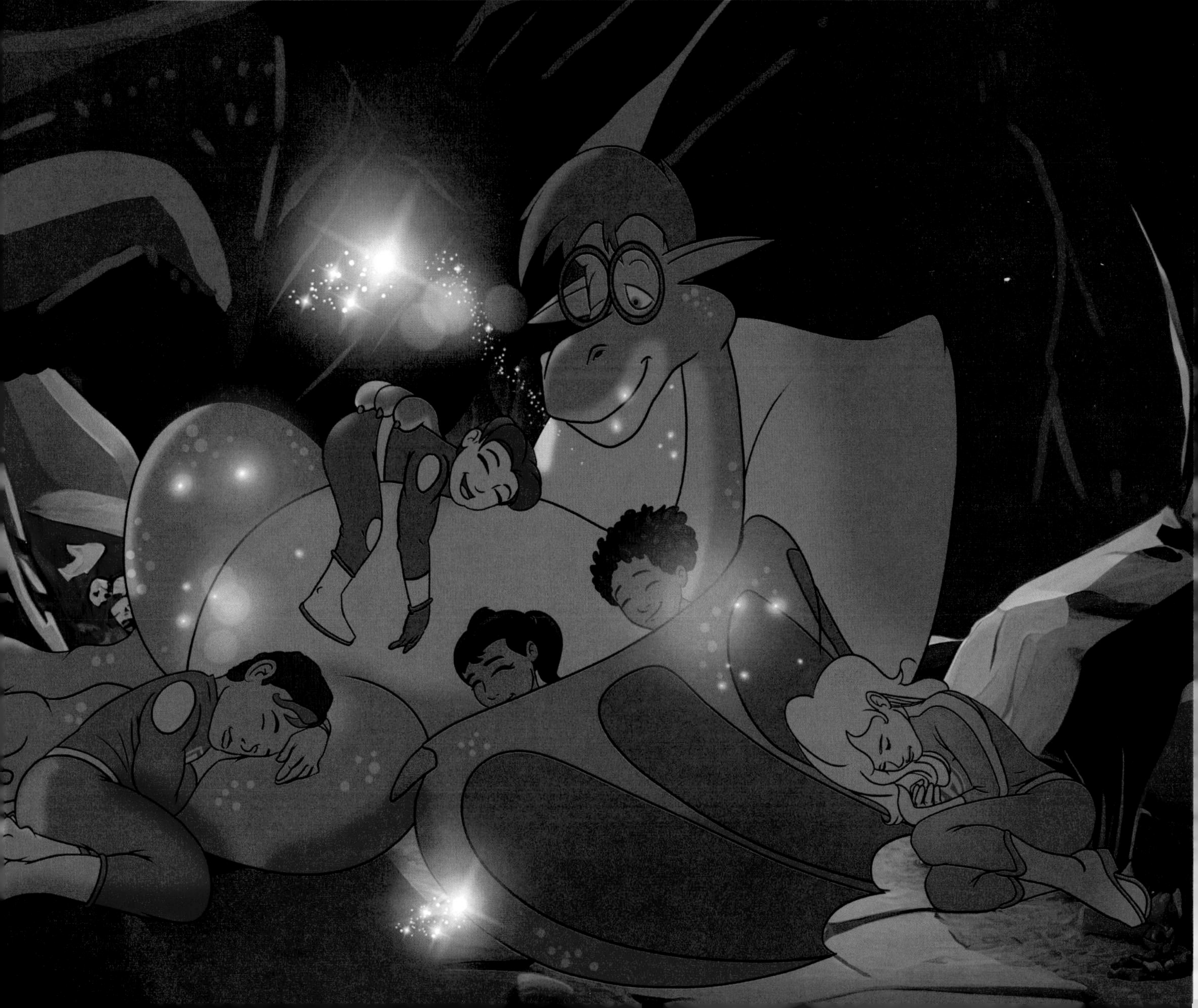

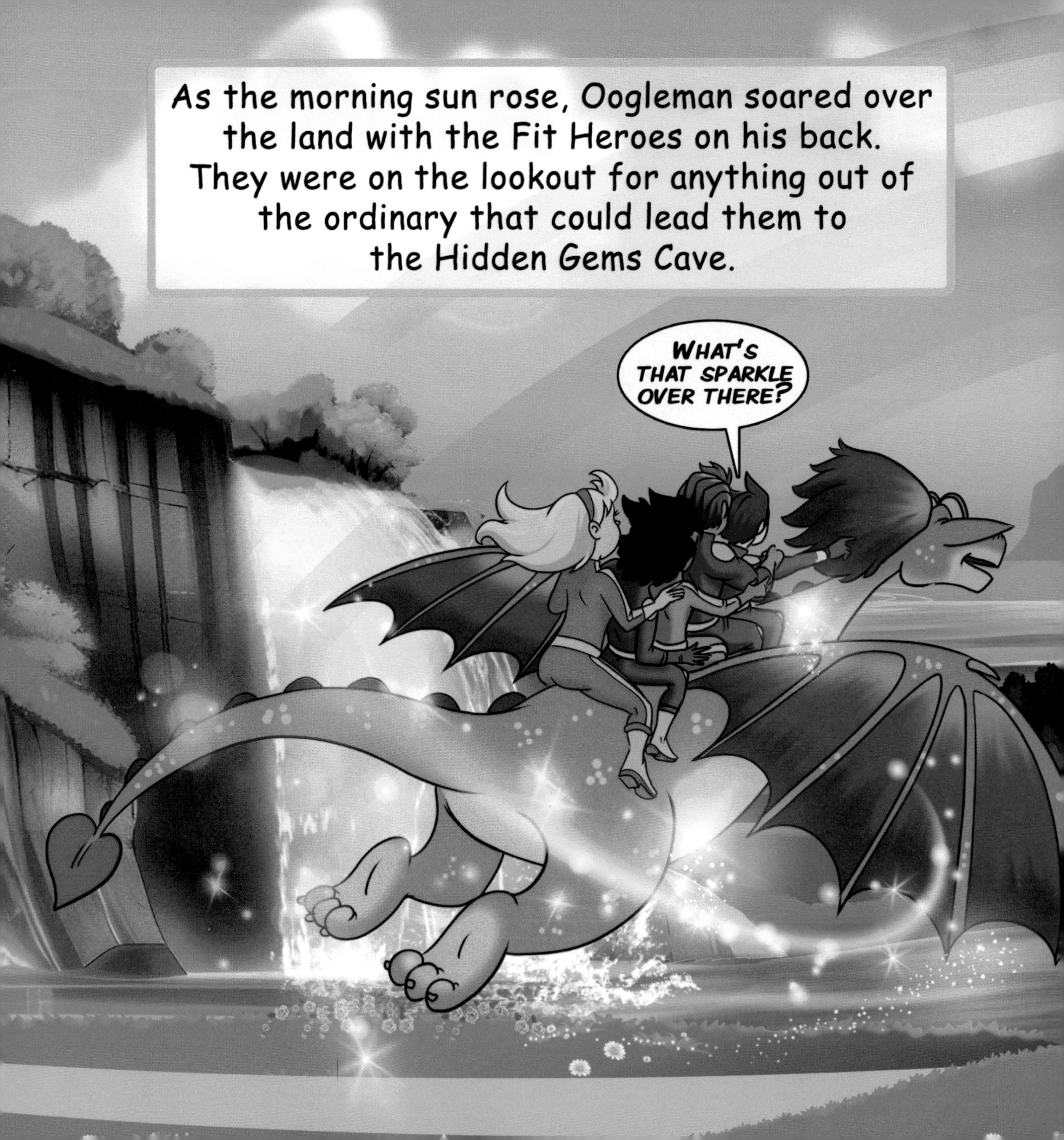
As the morning sun rose, Oogleman soared over the land with the Fit Heroes on his back. They were on the lookout for anything out of the ordinary that could lead them to the Hidden Gems Cave.
WHAT'S THAT SPARKLE OVER THERE?

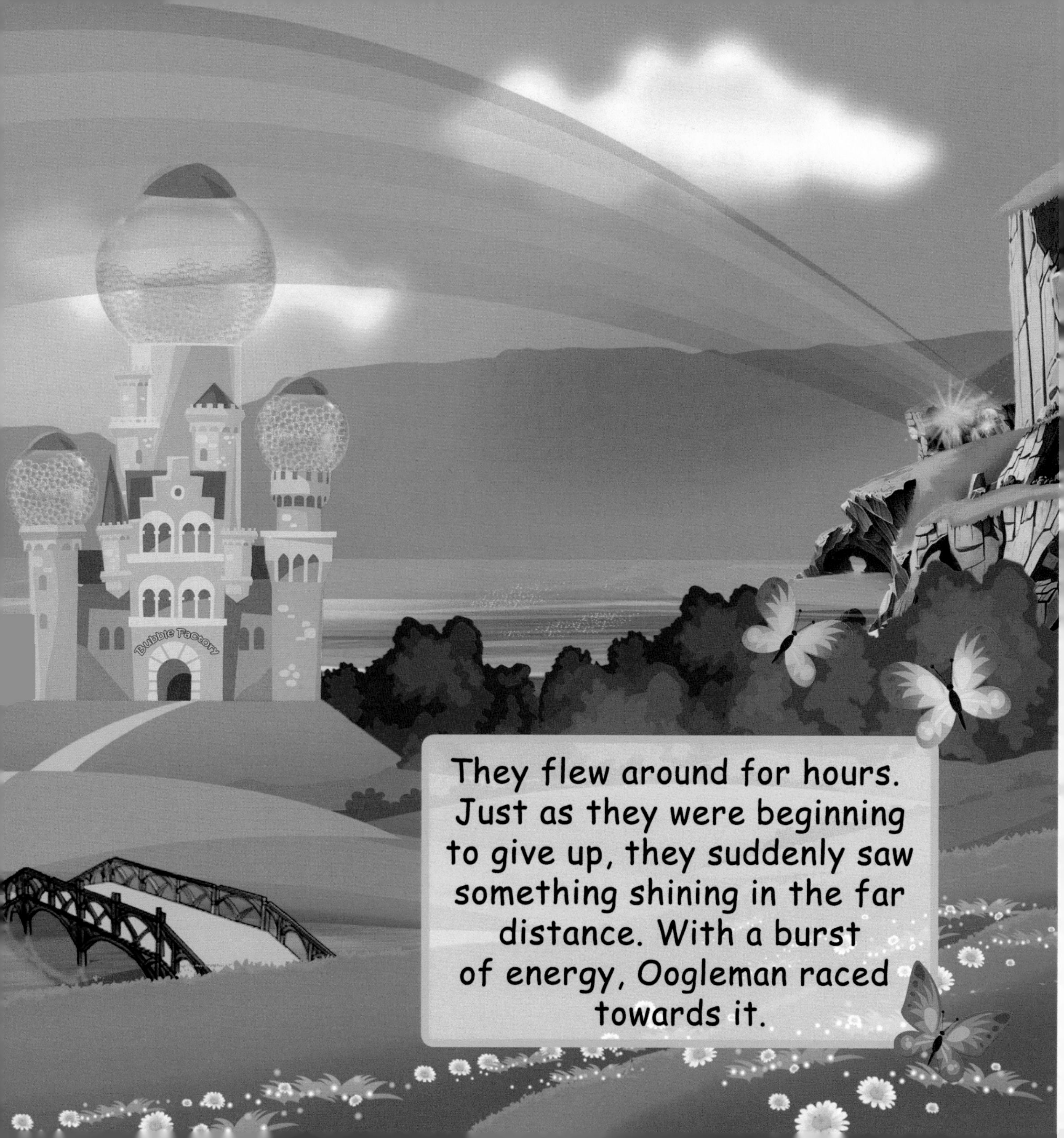
Bubble Factory

They flew around for hours. Just as they were beginning to give up, they suddenly saw something shining in the far distance. With a burst of energy, Oogleman raced towards it.

Their excitement surged as they got closer. Finally, they had found the Hidden Gems Cave!

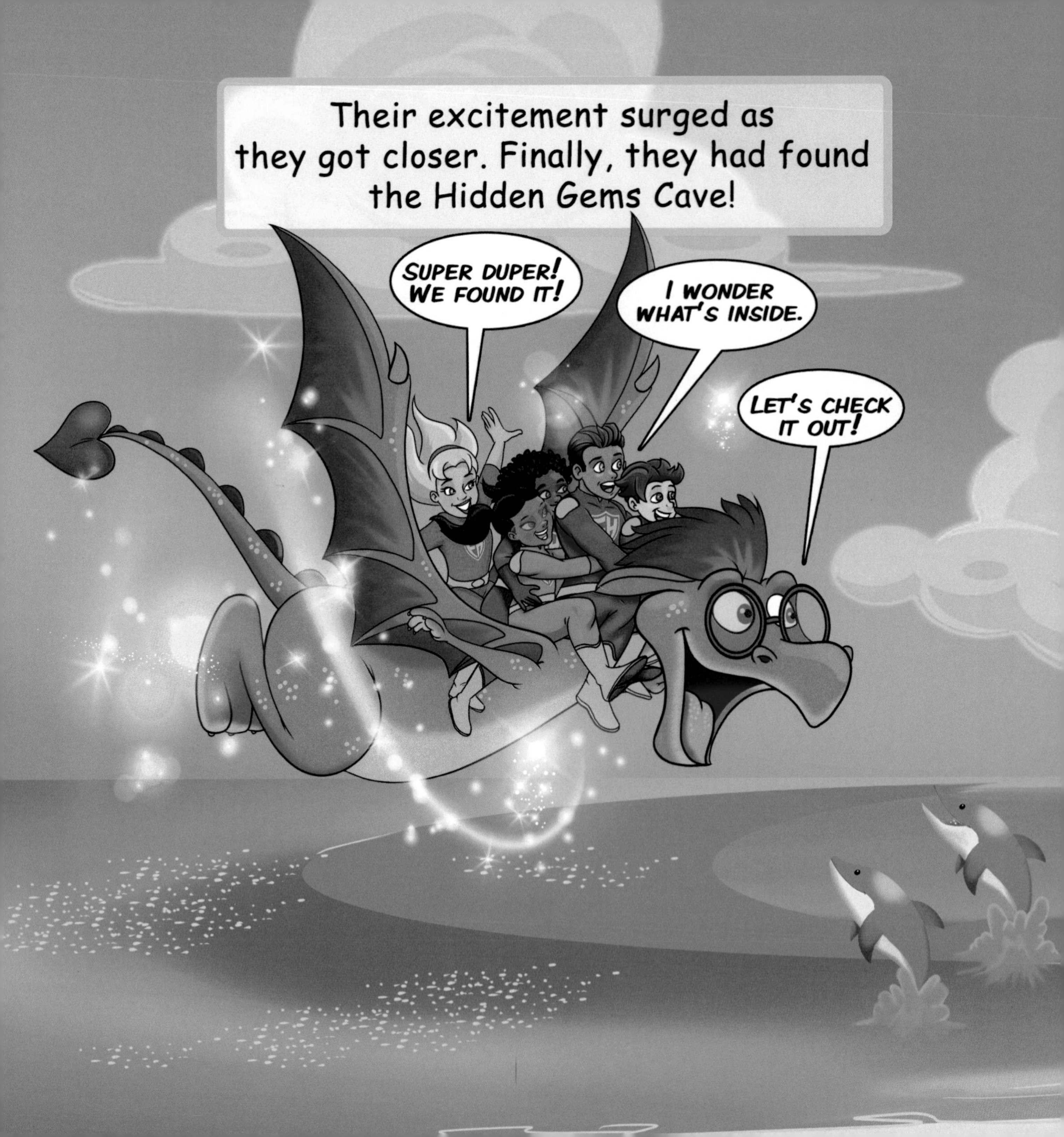
SUPER DUPER! WE FOUND IT!
I WONDER WHAT'S INSIDE.
LET'S CHECK IT OUT!

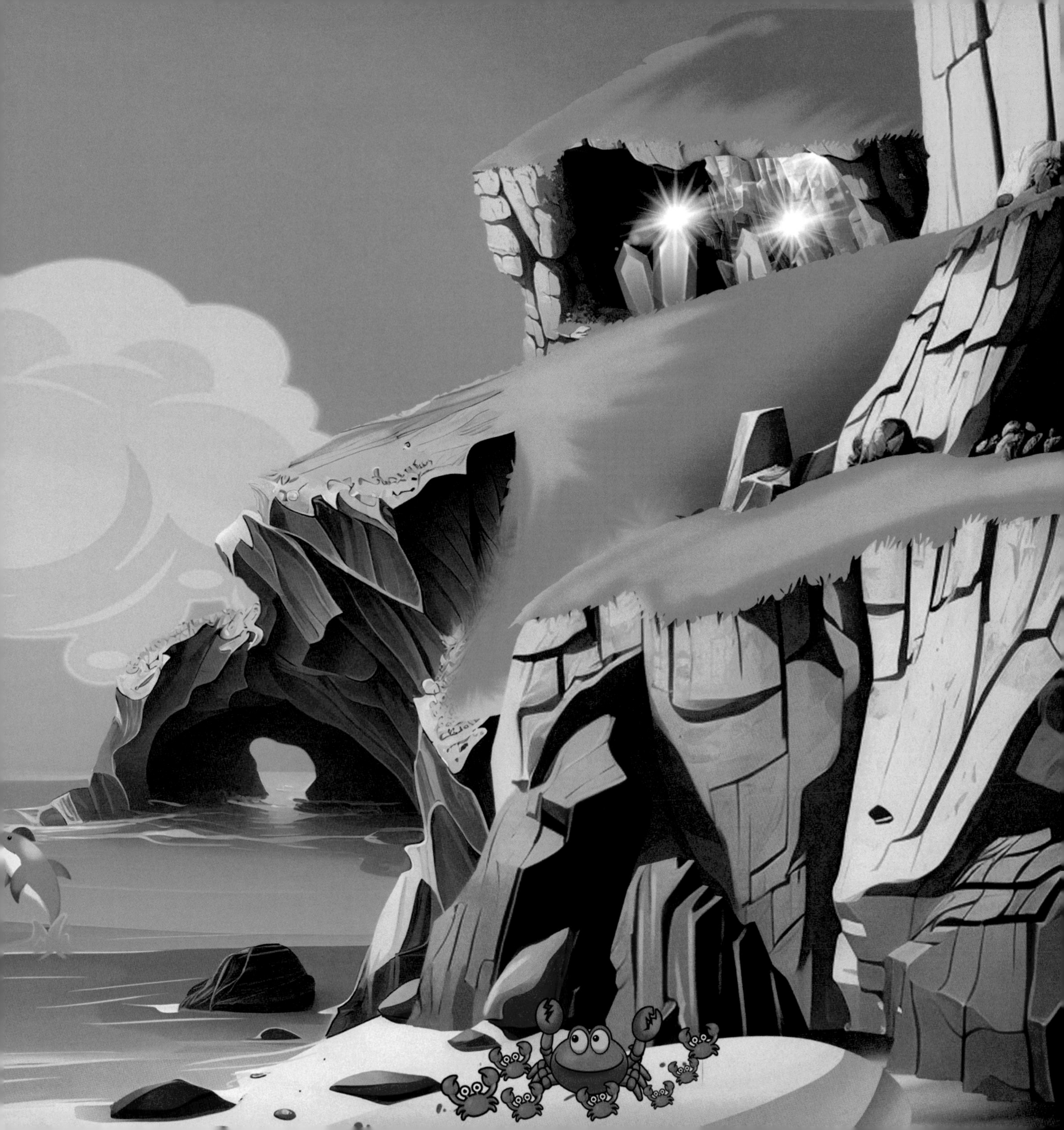

Oogleman and the Fit Heroes flew through the Hidden Gems Cave looking around in amazement at the colorful gemstones surrounding them. They could hardly wait to see what they would find at the end of the tunnel.

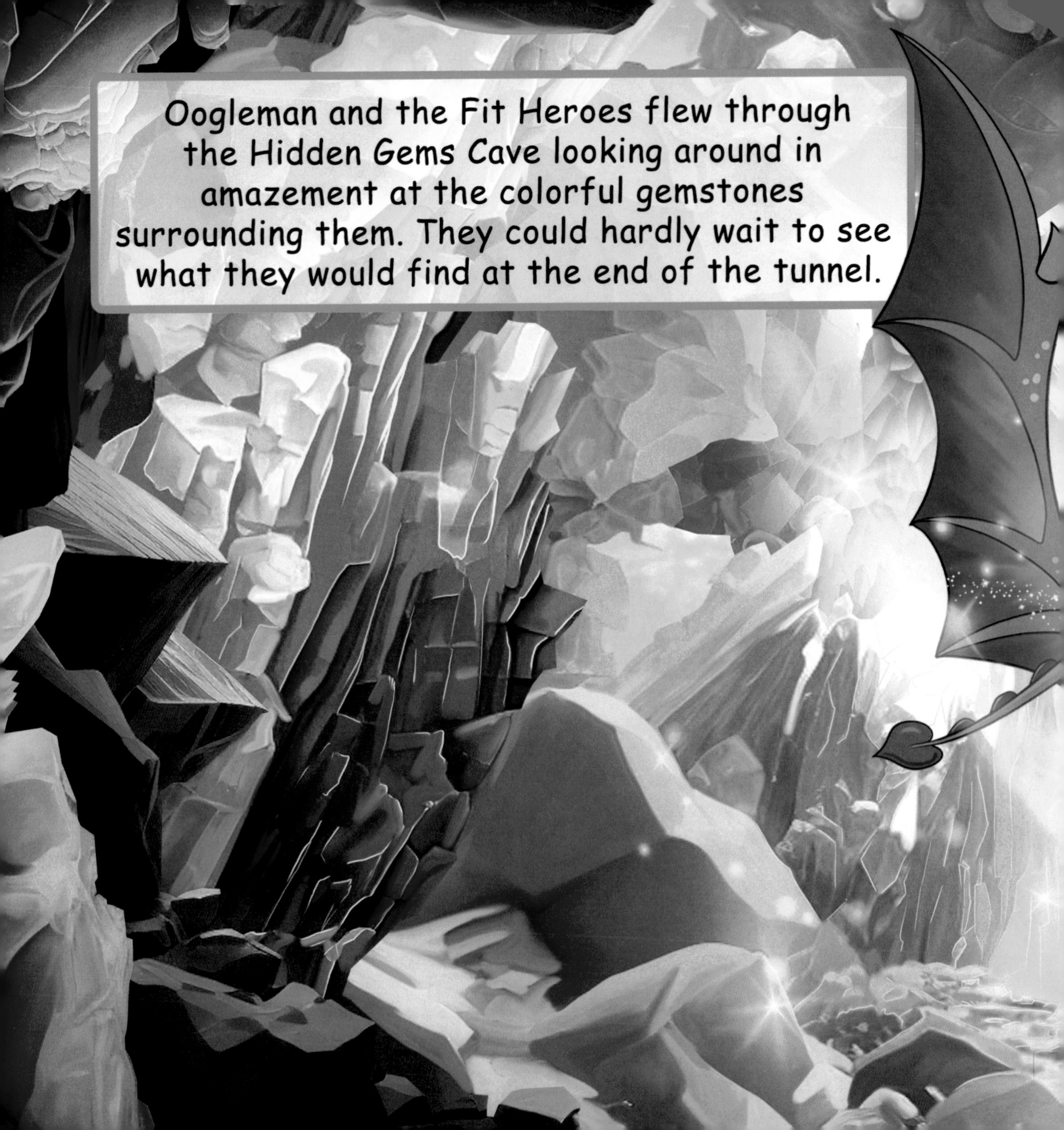

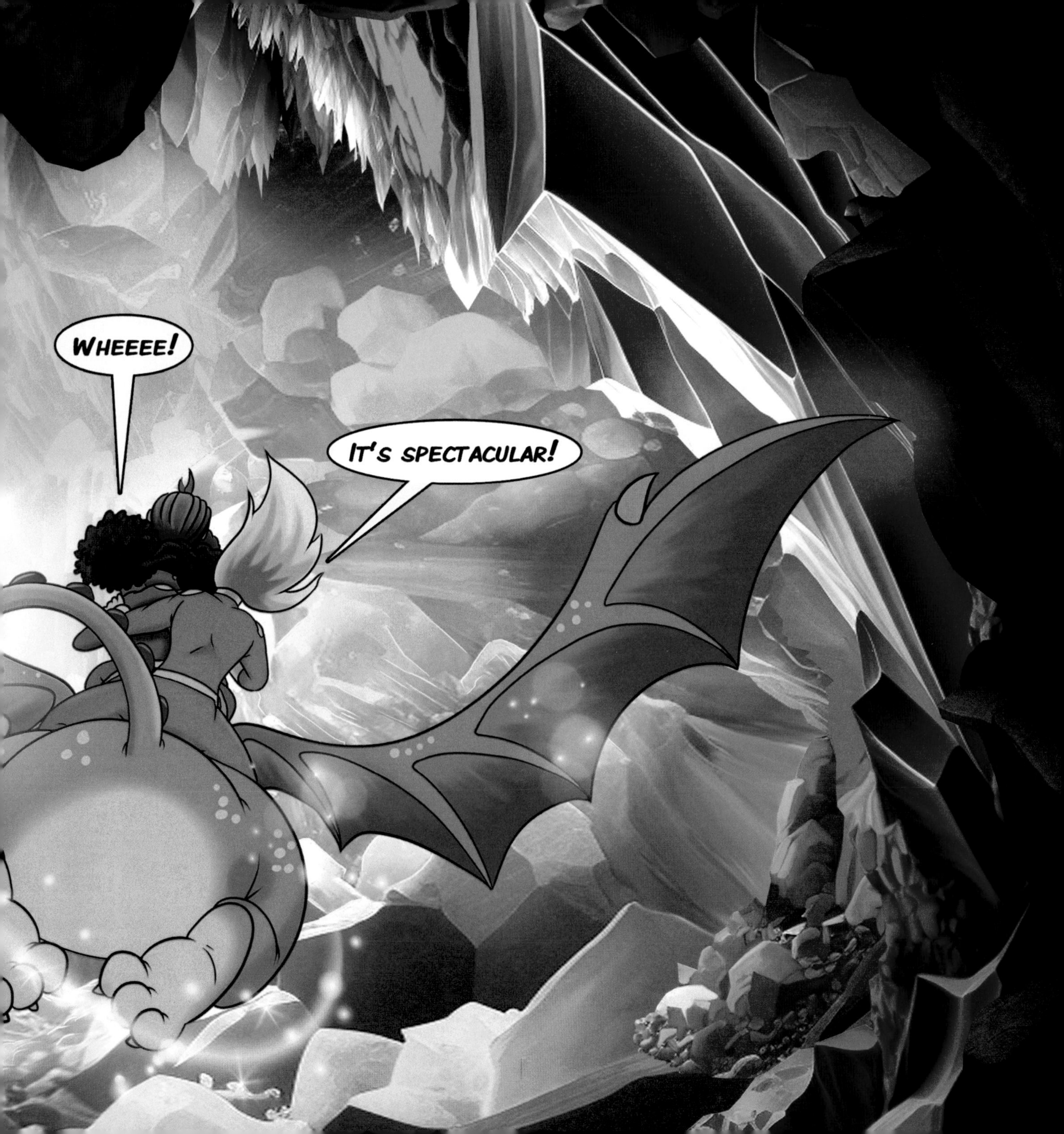
WHEEEE!
IT'S SPECTACULAR!

Suddenly, they came to a locked door. Around it were the words: "KIND, HELPFUL, LOVING, HONEST, CARING, and HEROIC." Only those who possessed those qualities could open it. They thought about how they could unlock this mysterious door.

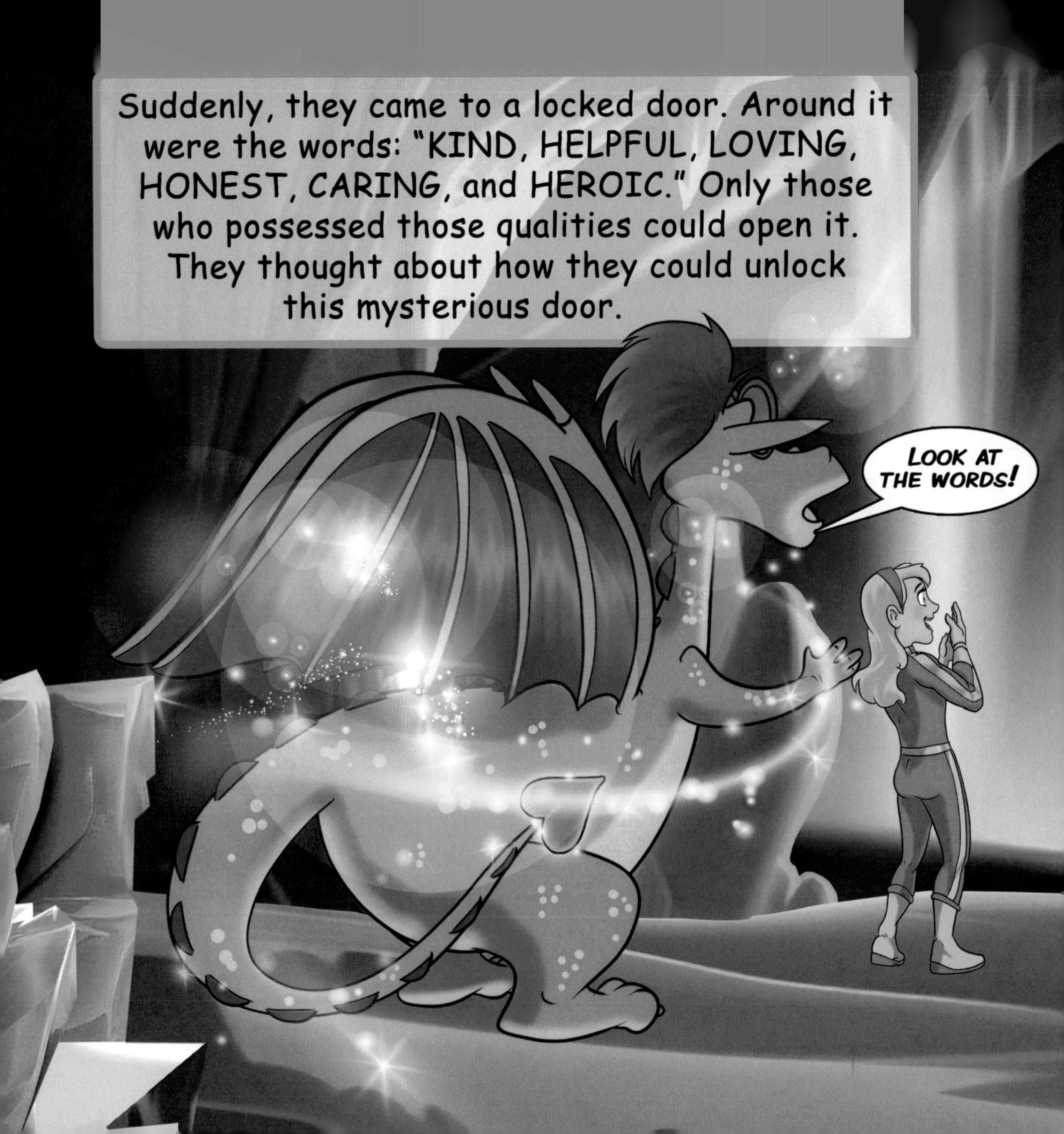
LOOK AT THE WORDS!

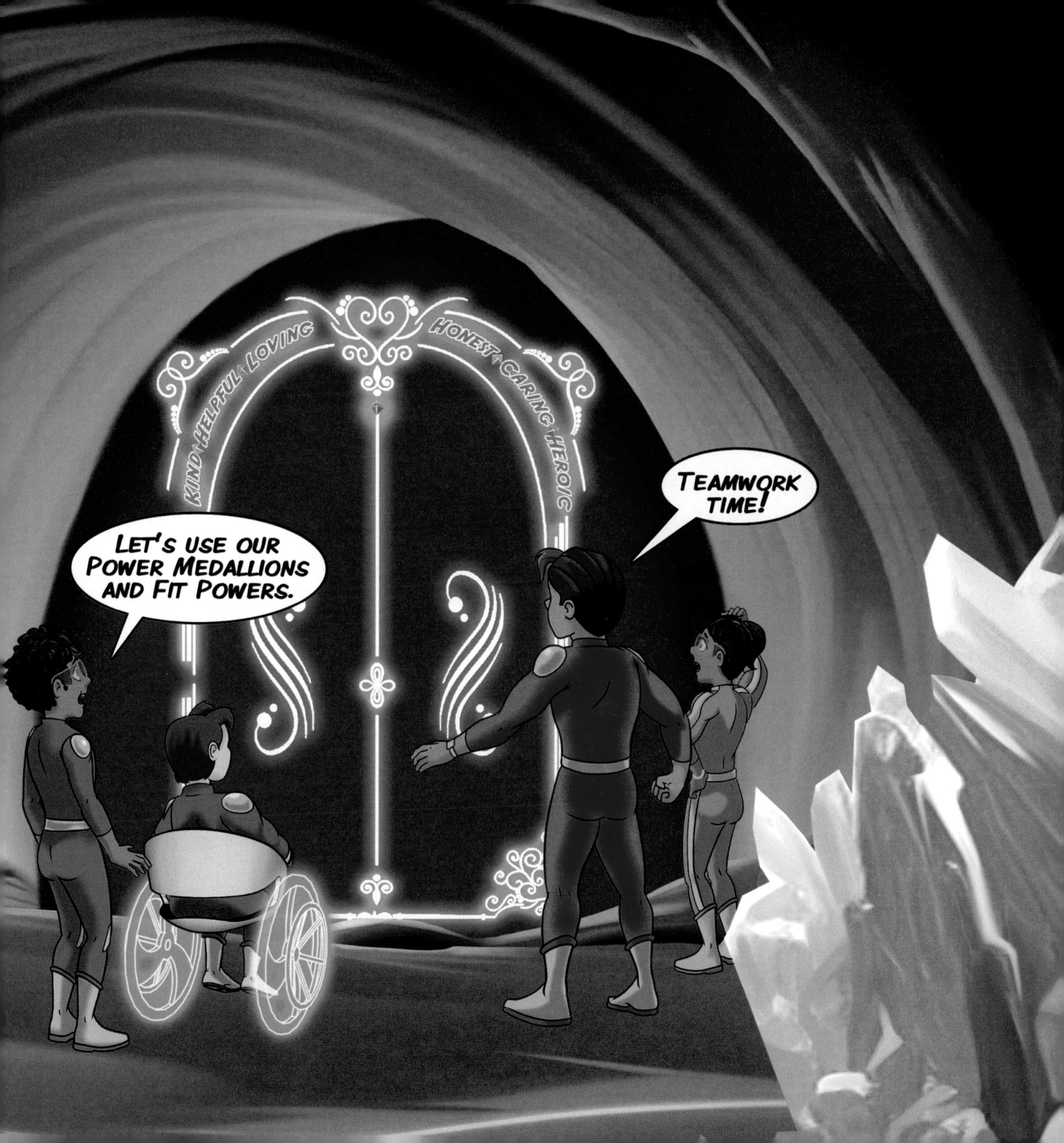
KIND HELPFUL LOVING
HONEST CARING HEROIC
LET'S USE OUR POWER MEDALLIONS AND FIT POWERS.
TEAMWORK TIME!

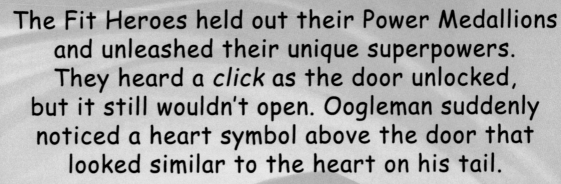

The Fit Heroes held out their Power Medallions and unleashed their unique superpowers. They heard a *click* as the door unlocked, but it still wouldn't open. Oogleman suddenly noticed a heart symbol above the door that looked similar to the heart on his tail.

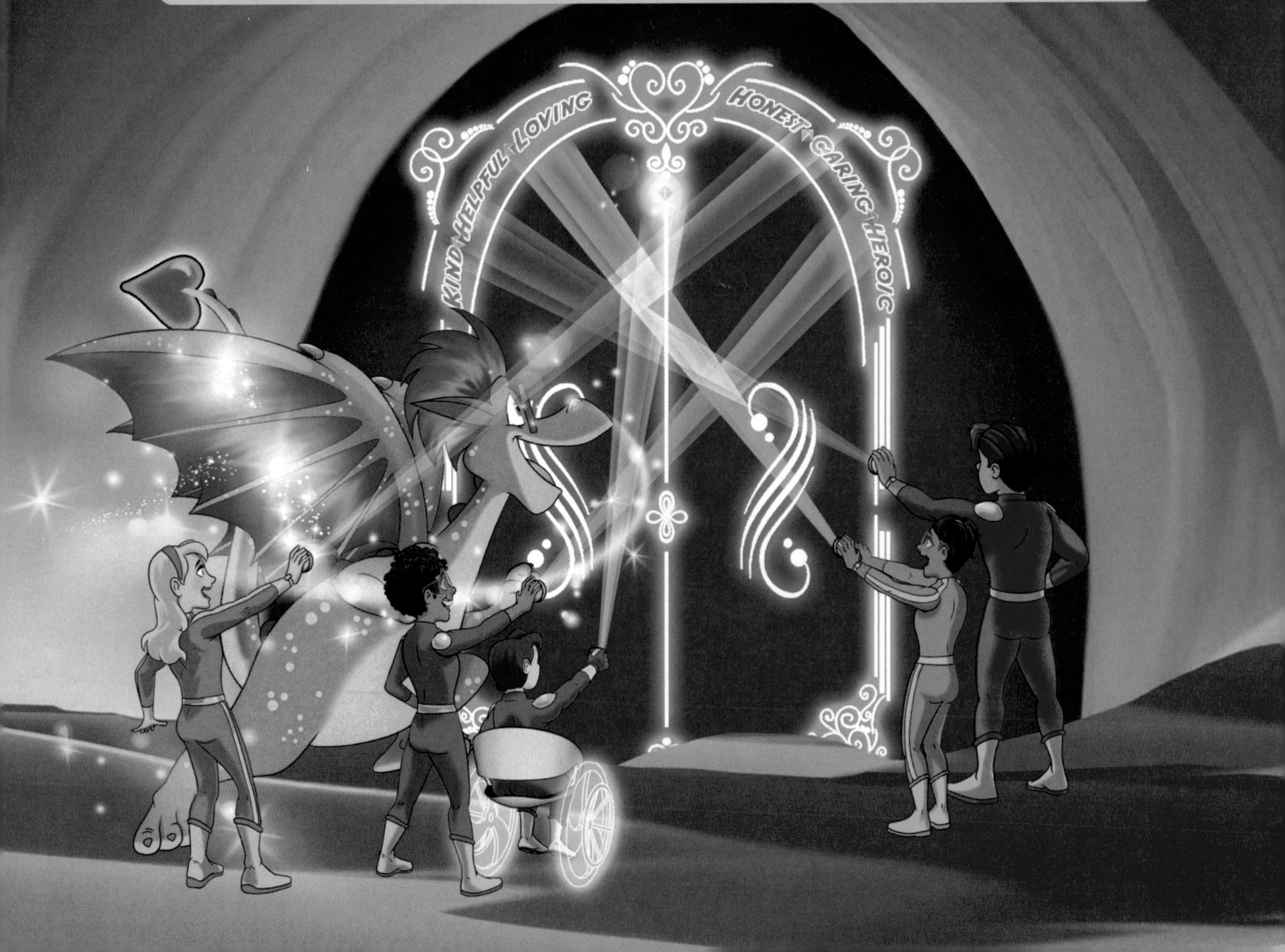
KIND
HELPFUL
LOVING
HONEST
CARING
HEROIC

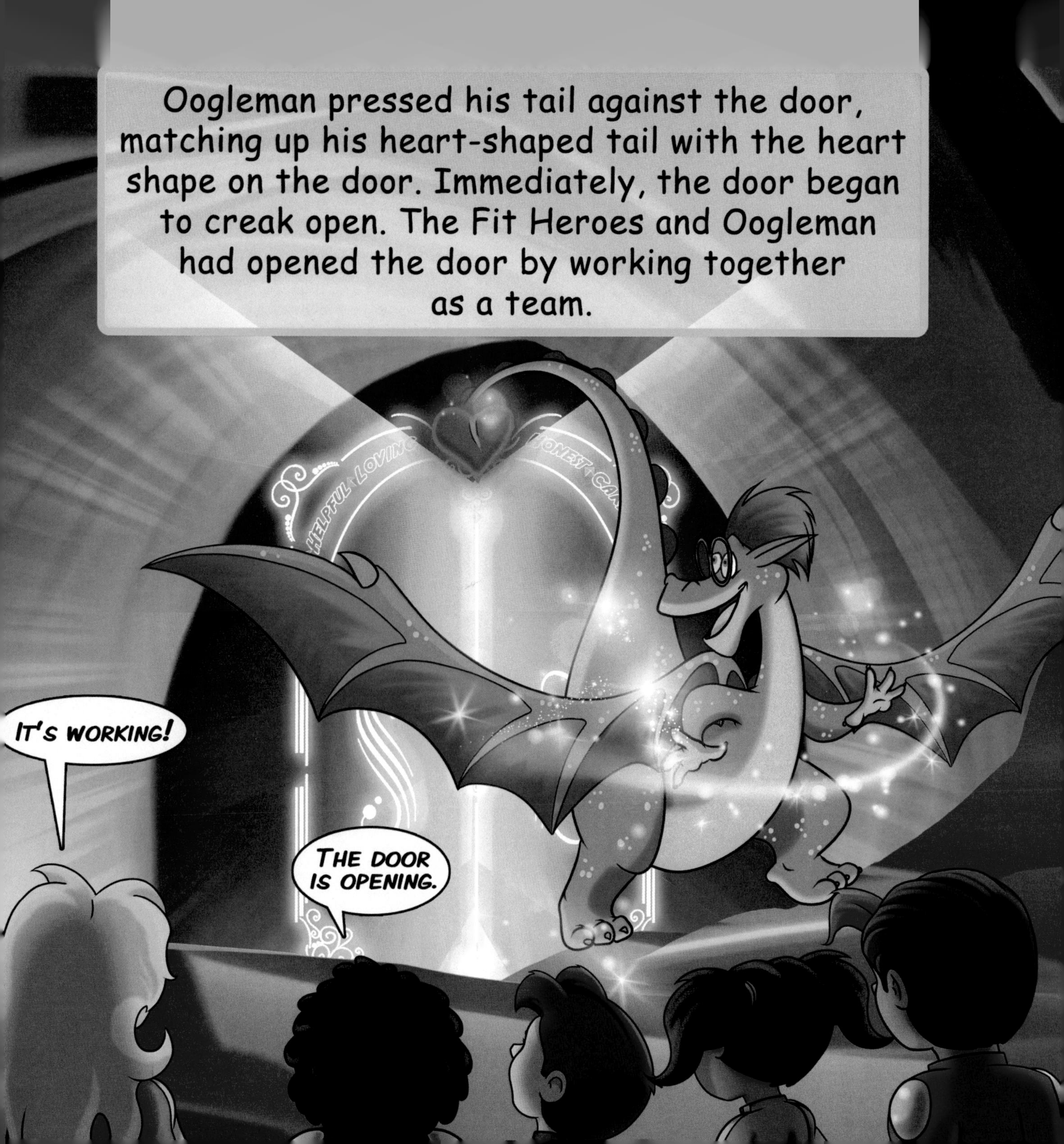
Oogleman pressed his tail against the door, matching up his heart-shaped tail with the heart shape on the door. Immediately, the door began to creak open. The Fit Heroes and Oogleman had opened the door by working together as a team.
HELPFUL
LOVING
HONEST
IT'S WORKING!
THE DOOR IS OPENING.

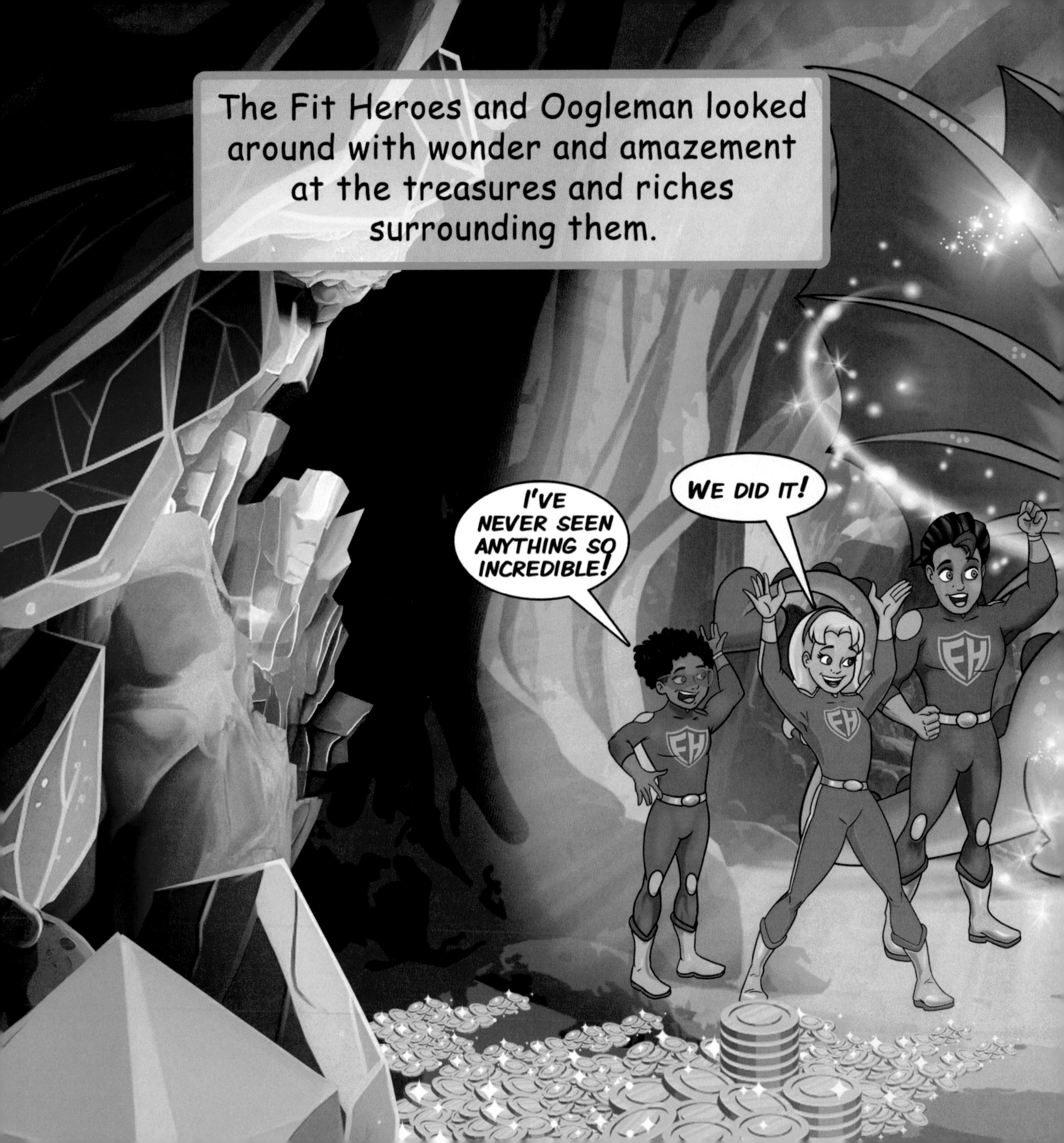
The Fit Heroes and Oogleman looked around with wonder and amazement at the treasures and riches surrounding them.
I'VE NEVER SEEN ANYTHING SO INCREDIBLE!
WE DID IT!

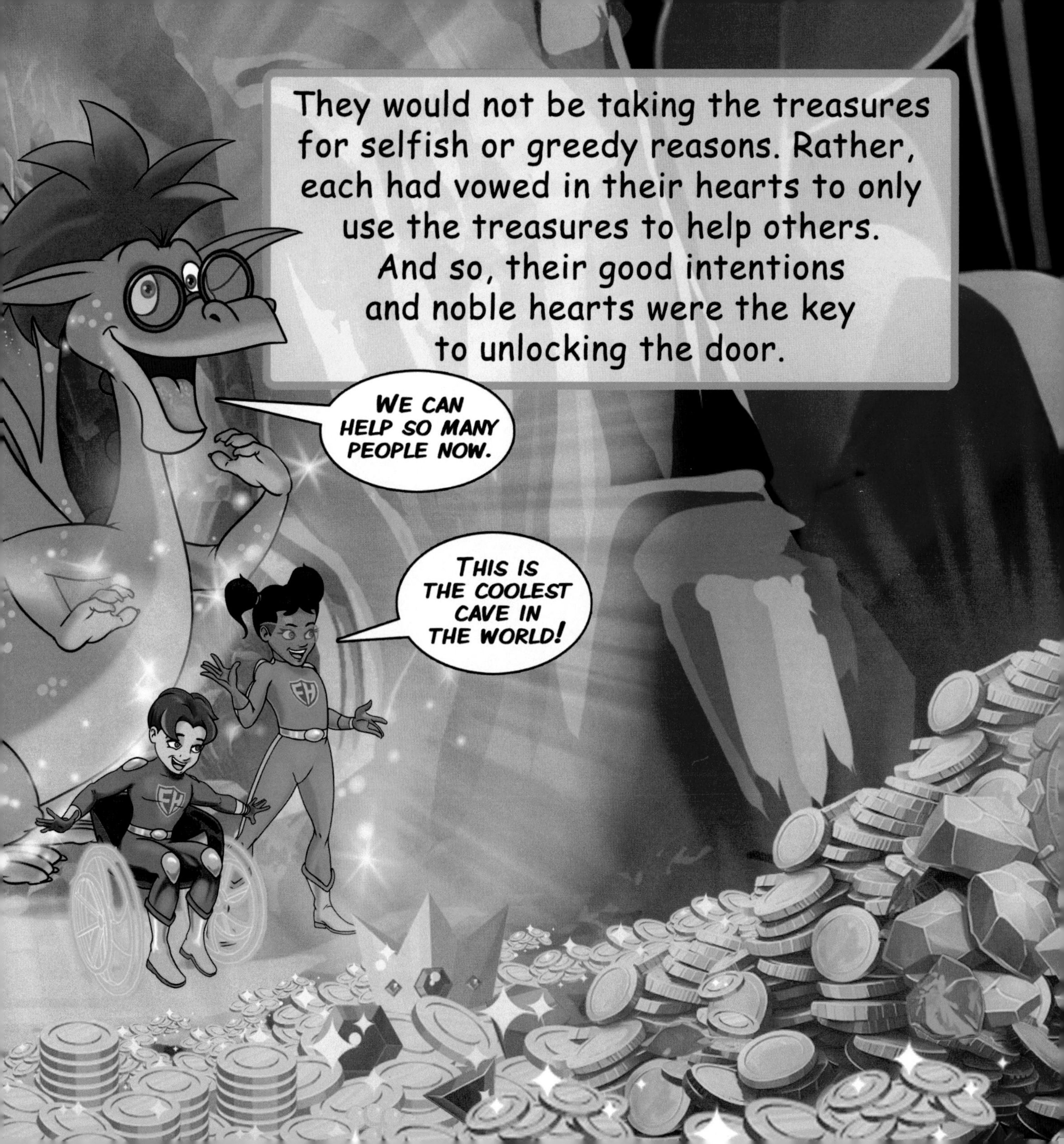
They would not be taking the treasures for selfish or greedy reasons. Rather, each had vowed in their hearts to only use the treasures to help others. And so, their good intentions and noble hearts were the key to unlocking the door.
WE CAN HELP SO MANY PEOPLE NOW.
THIS IS THE COOLEST CAVE IN THE WORLD!

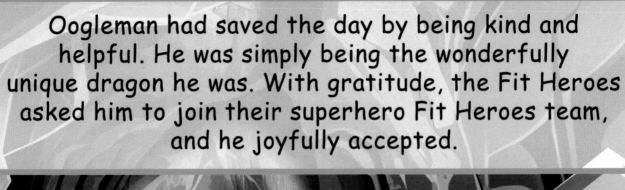

Oogleman had saved the day by being kind and helpful. He was simply being the wonderfully unique dragon he was. With gratitude, the Fit Heroes asked him to join their superhero Fit Heroes team, and he joyfully accepted.

Hooray! Oogleman was truly a Superhero Dragon in every way! He felt so loved and accepted by his new best friends, and he couldn't wait to go on more thrilling adventures with them.

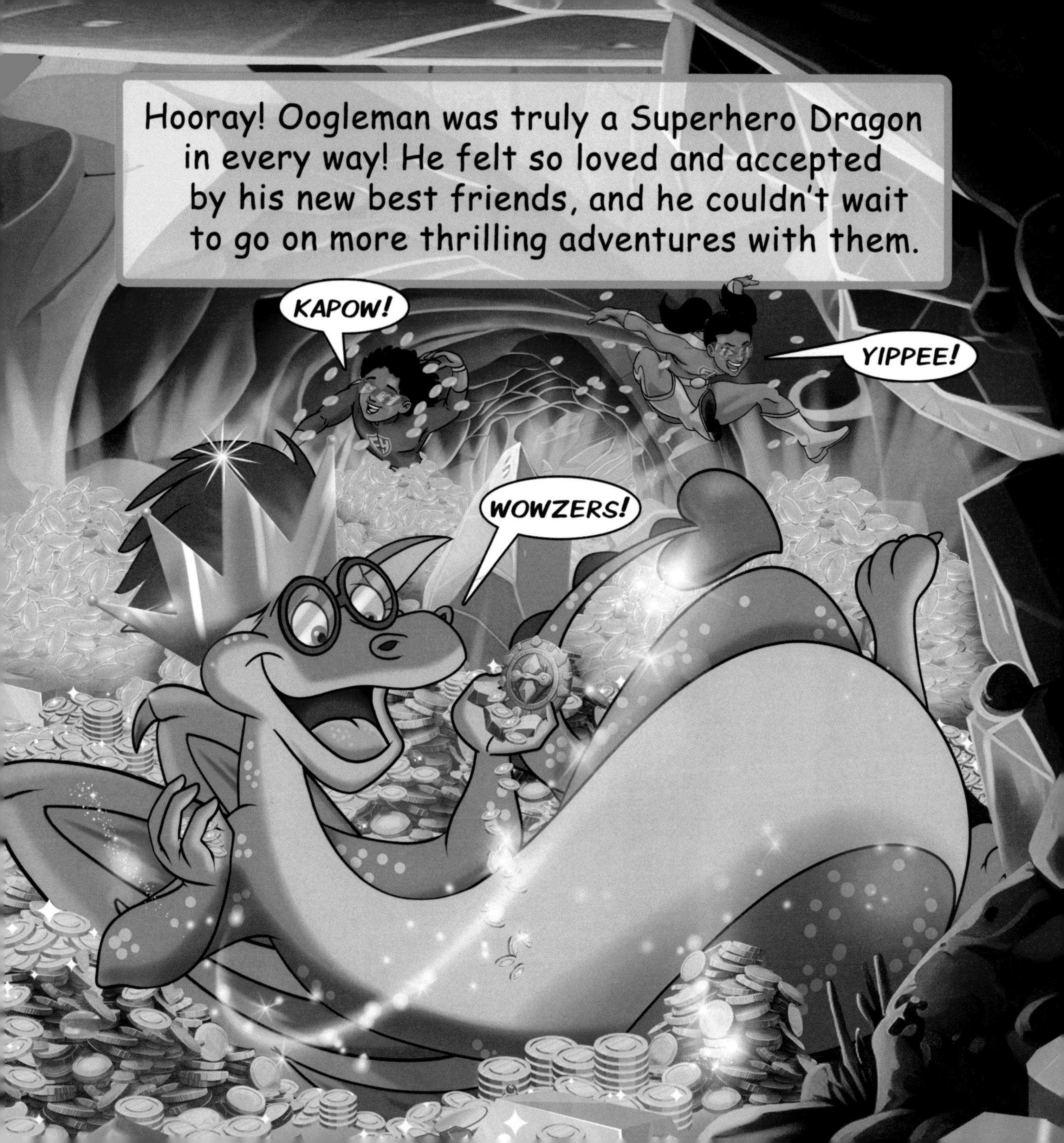
KAPOW!
YIPPEE!
WOWZERS!

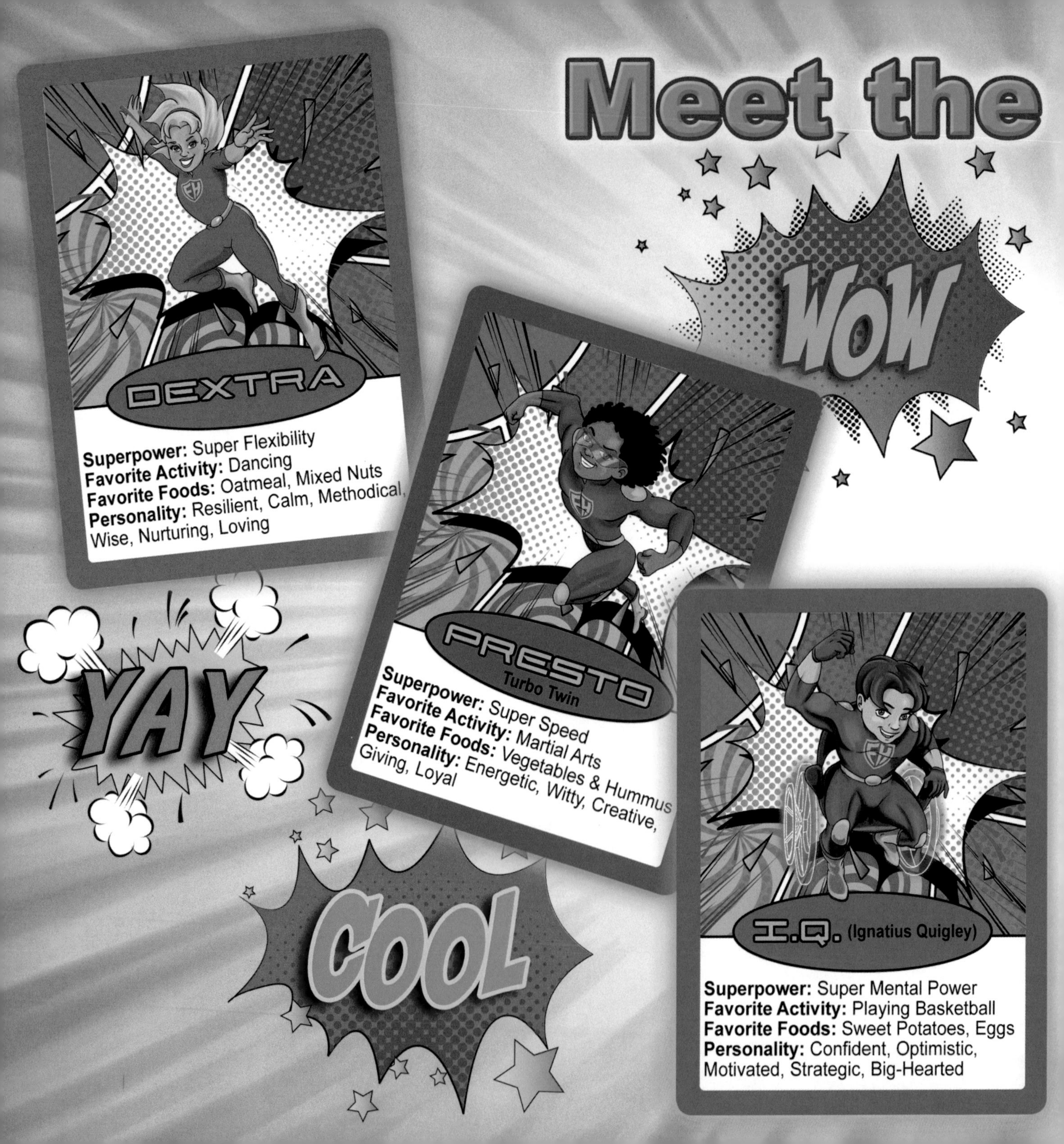

Meet the
WOW
DEXTRA
Superpower: Super Flexibility
Favorite Activity: Dancing
Favorite Foods: Oatmeal, Mixed Nuts
Personality: Resilient, Calm, Methodical, Wise, Nurturing, Loving
PRESTO
Turbo Twin
Superpower: Super Speed
Favorite Activity: Martial Arts
Favorite Foods: Vegetables & Hummus
Personality: Energetic, Witty, Creative, Giving, Loyal
I.Q. (Ignatius Quigley)
Superpower: Super Mental Power
Favorite Activity: Playing Basketball
Favorite Foods: Sweet Potatoes, Eggs
Personality: Confident, Optimistic, Motivated, Strategic, Big-Hearted
YAY
COOL

Fit Heroes

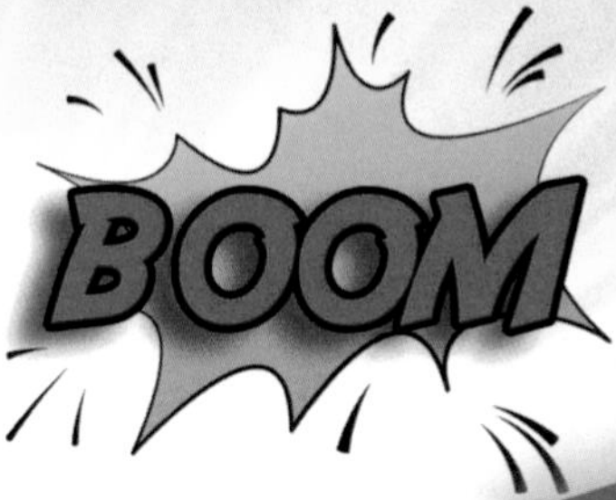
BOOM

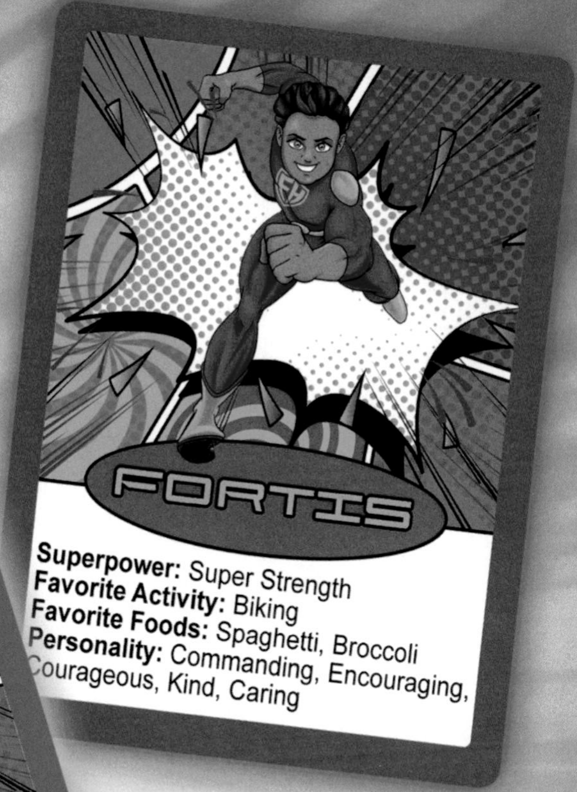
FORTIS
Superpower: Super Strength
Favorite Activity: Biking
Favorite Foods: Spaghetti, Broccoli
Personality: Commanding, Encouraging, Courageous, Kind, Caring

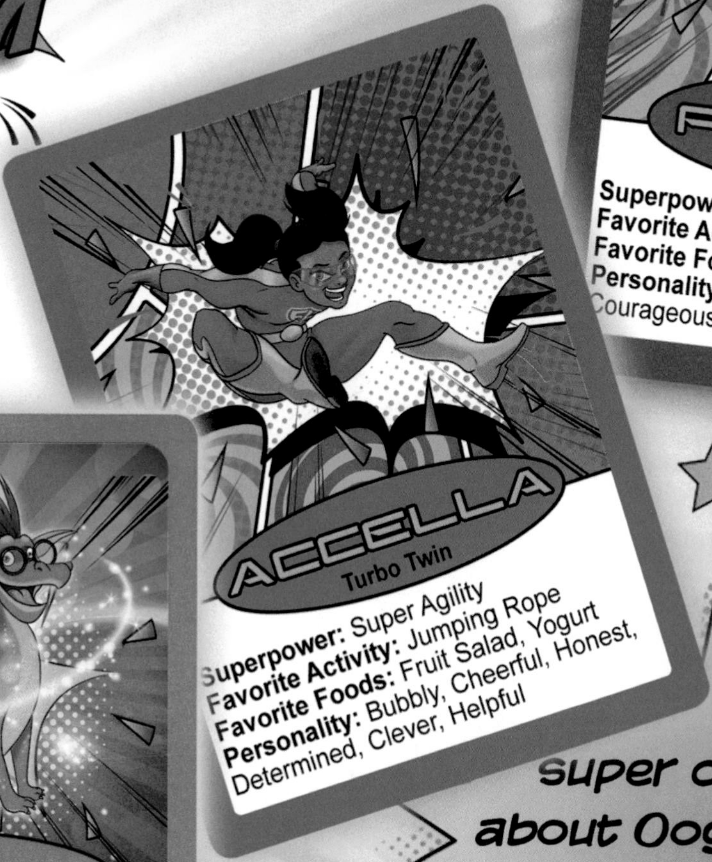
ACCELLA
Turbo Twin
Superpower: Super Agility
Favorite Activity: Jumping Rope
Favorite Foods: Fruit Salad, Yogurt
Personality: Bubbly, Cheerful, Honest, Determined, Clever, Helpful

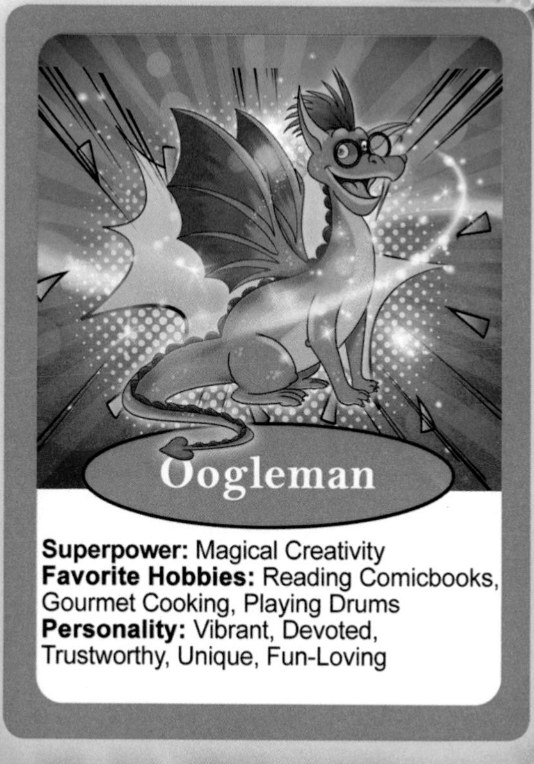
Oogleman
Superpower: Magical Creativity
Favorite Hobbies: Reading Comicbooks, Gourmet Cooking, Playing Drums
Personality: Vibrant, Devoted, Trustworthy, Unique, Fun-Loving

Check out super cool stuff about Oogleman and the Fit Heroes at:

www.FitHeroes.com

Never forget that your uniqueness is your special superpower!

You are a one-of-a-kind, real-life treasure. Let your love and kindness shine brightly...

The world needs your light.

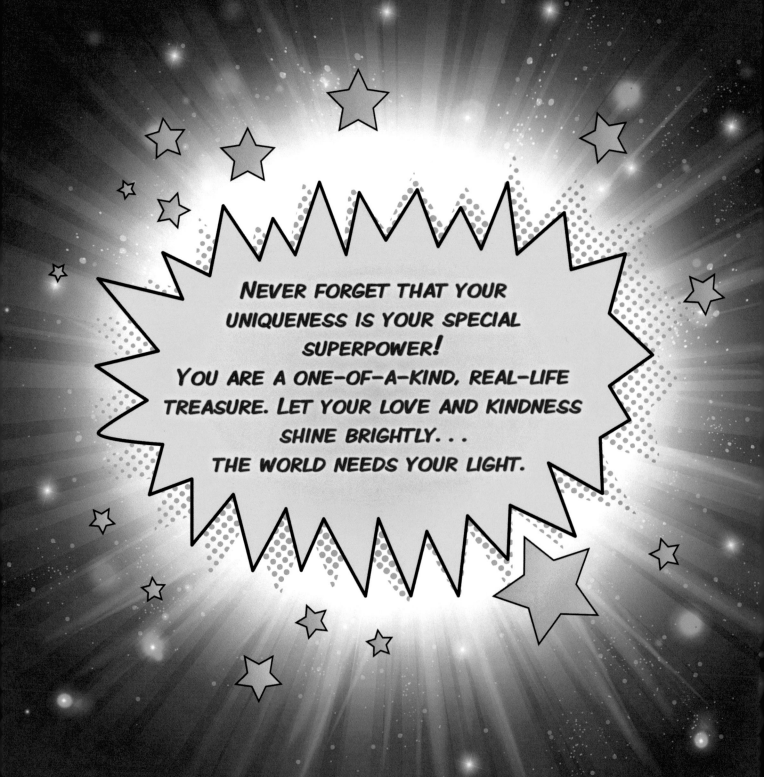

Made in the USA
Las Vegas, NV
08 July 2023

74333031R00021